The Architectural Cookbook

"Dinner is served, Madam."

The Architectural Cookbook

by ARTHUR HAWKINS

with illustrations by ALAN DUNN

ARCHITECTURAL RECORD BOOKS, *New York*

The editors for this book were Hugh S. Donlan and Martin Filler

The designer was Arthur Hawkins

The compositor was Publishers Compu-type Service, Inc.

The printer and binder were The Book Press

Copyright ©1975 by Architectural Record. All rights reserved. Printed in the United States of America. No part of this publication may be reproduced, stored in a retrieval system, or transmitted, in any form or by any means, electronic, mechanical, photocopying, recording, or otherwise, without the prior written permission of the publisher.

Library of Congress Catalogue Card Number: 75-5090

Published by Architectural Record, A McGraw-Hill Publication, 1221 Avenue of the Americas, New York, New York 10020

FOREWORD

This is not a "run-of-the-kitchen" cookbook! Not only do the recipes represent a pluralism of culinary styles symptomatic of the contemporary scene, but here, for the first time, *gastronomy is brought to the service of the built environment!*

Curious that heretofore no attempt has been made to bridge the gap between the groaning board and the drawing board. Does not the palate lie closer to the cerebral hemispheres (the seat of environmental planning) than to the stomach?

A cookbook for architects, engineers, contractors, and all who love good architecture should be more than a gallimaufry of sybaritic dishes, more than a placation of clamorous taste buds.

It should be as well a paean of praise and a source of inspiration—fueling the creative spirit as it subdues the appetite.

À la table!

Let knife and fork close ranks with t-squares and dividers! "He who would build better must eat better!"

    Blake Hughes
    Publisher
    Architectural Record
    January 1975

CONTENTS

	FOREWORD BY BLAKE HUGHES
8	INTRODUCTION BY WALTER F. WAGNER, JR.
11	1. HORS D'OEUVRES AND SNACKS
19	2. SOUPS AND STEWS
31	3. EGGS, CHEESES AND PASTA
43	4. MEATS
65	5. POULTRY AND SEAFOOD
87	6. VEGETABLES AND SIDE DISHES
93	7. SAUCES AND DRESSINGS
99	8. DESSERTS AND SWEETS
113	9. BREADS, CAKES AND COOKIES
123	10. BEVERAGES
133	MENUS

INTRODUCTION

In its 84 years of publication, ARCHITECTURAL RECORD has published over 1000 issues. This is our first cookbook. It will undoubtedly be our last, because as the great gourmet Nero said in A.D. LXVII . . .

Ubi vidisti unum librum de arte coquinaria architectonicum, vidisti eos omnes[1]

What business, you may ask, does a responsible professional architectural magazine have publishing a cookbook?
 None whatever.
 How then, you may ask, do I happen to find myself with a copy of this book?
 By an extraordinary series of circumstances.
 It all started when Blake Hughes, publisher of ARCHITECTURAL RECORD, had a kind of stomach-storm (which is two feet below a brain storm) and invited Arthur Hawkins, his favorite guide to culinary delights and a long-time free-lance designer for RECORD, to do an architectural cookbook. What he proposed was a kind of "love feast" cookbook—one that would cause architects, engineers, contractors, and builders to rejoice together. It would be a cookbook for all who love good architecture and good food. (Hence our title.)
 Drooling over this improbable proposal, his great moustache bristling, Hawkins—superb chef, innovative developer of new recipes, and author of 12 cookbooks which have been highly praised by *The New York Times, The Bergen (N.J.) Record*, and such *grands gourmets* as the school-lunch menu editor of the *Frisbee (New Hampshire) Town Crier*—retired to contemplate this challenge.

[1]Shame on you! Go back and work it out. If you can't:
 If you've seen one architectural cookbook, you've seen 'em all.

At that point, as often, the editors of RECORD were called in to work out a few small details. Like why would professional practitioners buy a cookbook? How could it be presented in a way so appealing that all architects would buy a copy, and at the same time be sufficiently general in nature that everyone else who loves good architecture would, too?

The editors promptly mounted a massive research program (it was at lunch one day) which revealed that an extraordinary percentage of architects:

1. Own Porsche automobiles (though with the shifting emphasis from design to comprehensive service, Mercedes-Benz 450 SLs are moving in);

2. Sail and ski (a nice combination of esthetically pleasing equipment, movement, and environment).

3. Have great-looking wives and/or girl friends, and . . .

4. Eat.

Indeed, many think of eating as a mother art—akin, say, to architecture. "And this correlation between eating and architecture," our research report concluded, "clearly justifies RECORD publishing a cookbook [neat reasoning, eh?]".

There was another teensy problem. This had been conceived as a humorous cookbook—"giving names to each dish that would be architecturally appropriate." The trouble was that funniest ideas around were Arthur's Cantilever Cake (both words start with C, see?), Split-level Soup (ditto, get it?) and Fried Systems. Question: Could the editors think up a few funnier names?

Well, the standard for that sort of thing had been set at a very high level by Lolly McDonnell-Mitchell and a few of her Cambridge (Mass.) friends, who formed the Lone Star Publishing Company of Boston to publish "The Watergate Cookbook—Or Who's in the Soup". I mean Nixon's Perfectly Clear Consomme or Ellsberg's Leek Soup or Martha's Sweet and Sour Tongue have style and class.

Undaunted, the editors (with the tireless help of the circulation department, the book department, visiting architects, messengers from the printer and photostaters passing through the office, and my son the architecture student) bent to the task.

We quickly accelerated from such obviousities as Tea Squares and I Beans into esoterica. I mean Eternal Ziti really brings new grandeur to Italian cuisine. Vierend Eel is so high-pitched only structural engineers can hear it. (See, a Vierendeel is a truss having rigid joints between the verticals and the chords and . . .

9

ah, never mind.) And not totally respectful uses of the names of distinguished professionals poured forth in profusion. We quickly passed through such simplicities as Franks Lloyd Wright and McKim, Mead and White Sauce into Gropius TACos and Inigo Scones.

Some professionals thus enshrined insisted on taking part in "their" recipe. Architectural photographer Ezra Stoller, for instance, ensured the memorability of Ezra Stollen by suggesting that "with the almonds, citron, etc. be added ⅓ cup white wine, ⅓ cup black raisins and, to help 'develop' it, 4 teaspoons of anisette liquer."

Confronted with Plat Nerwarren, architect Warren Platner admitted to "some dismay at possible blanching, parboiling, skinning, poaching, and decanting. On the other hand," said he, "clarifying may be what I need most."

And engineer Bill LeMessurier wrote: "You have my complete permission to christen a dish Lamb LeMessurier. My only reservation is that it must not be overcooked. No Frenchman would ever eat anything but pink lamb."

He suggested, as many did, another dish. "This being the venison season in New England, I suggest Hart a la TAC." Phil Meathe of Smith, Hinchman & Grylls (Smith, Hinchman Mixed Gryll, inevitably) suggested a number of others: "For outdoor barbeques, Whole Roast Bullock [Tom Bullock is the president of CRS and a major competitor of Phil's], and that famous Pennsylvania Dutch dish, Apple Pan Dow [as in Alden Dow of Midland, Michigan] [rejected only because we already had Apple Pan Gaudi]."

Our only real disappointment is that we couldn't come up with a recipe using a totally unbent and unblemished name. Mies van der Roe comes pretty close. But the ultimate—Wolf Von Eckardt—foundered on a simple scarcity of the key ingredient. Thus the distinguished architectural critic of *The Washington Post* is memorialized with mere Von Eckardt Boiled Eggs (Eckardt....Hardt....Hard....Hard Boiled....get it?) Ah, nuts.
. . . Walnuts?
. . . Walnuts?
   Walter
   Walter Wagner, AIA
   Editor, Architectural Record
   Artichokes al Record?
   January 1975

Hors d'Oeuvres and Snacks

"Dinner will be slightly delayed—jammed partition."

Horta d'Oeuvres

Horta d'Oeuvres originally were served as a first dinner course to be eaten with fork, but more recently they have taken the form of finger food at cocktail parties. The variety of such snacks is almost endless, ranging from cooked meats and seafood to raw cheeses, vegetables, and nuts. Here are a few to get you started:

Mash cream cheese, season to taste, shape into small balls, and roll in crushed potato chips.

Mash cream cheese, dust with paprika, and roll in slices of chipped beef.

Pour part of the brine from a bottle of stuffed olives, add a cut clove of garlic and a little lime juice, and let stand for a day or so.

Sauté salted peanuts in butter sprinkled with curry powder.

Stuff celery stalks with a mixture of blue cheese, mayonnaise, and sour cream.

Season hamburger with mustard, salt, and pepper, and form into small balls. Sauté in oil and serve on toothpicks.

Wrap cocktail frankfurters (or sliced frankfurters) with bacon, fasten with toothpicks, and sauté in hot oil.

Cut hard-cooked eggs in half lengthwise, remove the yolks, and fill the whites with tuna fish or deviled ham; dab with mayonnaise and sprinkle with crumbled egg yolks.

Brush pork spareribs with a mixture of honey and Worcestershire, and broil in the oven until crisp.

Pâté Maison Carrée

1 pound chicken livers (or goose livers), coarsely chopped
¼ green pepper, minced
1 medium onion, minced
3 tablespoons olive oil (or butter)
2 slices white bread, soaked in milk and pressed dry
2 hard-cooked eggs, chopped
2 teaspoons salt
1 teaspoon pepper
1 teaspoon paprika
few grains cayenne

Sauté the livers, green pepper, and onion in the oil for 2 minutes. Remove from the heat and mix well with the bread, eggs, and seasonings.

Put through a food grinder twice, check for seasoning, form into a brick or carrée, and refrigerate.

Slice and serve cold.

6 TO 8 SERVINGS

Cul-de-Snack

1 Edam cheese
Roquefort cheese
butter, softened
Worcestershire sauce
brandy

Scoop out the center of the Edam, and mix with an equal amount of Roquefort cheese and half as much butter. Season to taste with Worcestershire and/or brandy. Stuff back into the Edam shell.

Park Avenue Canopies

Canopies are tiny open sandwiches spread with a meat, fish, or cheese mixture and served at cocktail time. The base may be a thin triangle or round of buttered bread (toasted or not) or a crisp cracker.

Park Avenue canopies are usually garnished with a dash of paprika, a bit of parsley, or a slice of olive or lemon.

A few interesting spreads are given below. These should inspire you to invent your own.

Spread #1: Mix together anchovy paste, finely chopped hard-cooked eggs, mayonnaise, and a few drops of Tabasco sauce.

Spread #2: Mix together finely chopped green olives, finely chopped ripe olives, sour cream, and a pinch of curry powder.

Spread #3: Mix together finely chopped pimentoes finely chopped onion, sour cream and a little chili powder.

Spread #4: Mix together kippered herring, horseradish, mayonnaise, salt and pepper.

Spread #5: Mix together cream cheese, red caviar, and a few dashes of Worcestershire sauce.

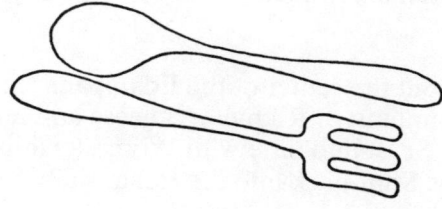

Catenary Dip

1 small package cream cheese
1 teaspoon grated onion
1 teaspoon chopped and mashed anchovies
2 teaspoons capers
2 dashes Worcestershire sauce

Mix all the ingredients together thoroughly, thin to desired consistency with cream, mayonnaise, or a combination of both.

Place into a bowl in the center of a serving tray and surround with potato chips, Melba toast, crackers, corn chips, raw bits of cauliflower, sticks of celery, or carrots.

Pizza Piazza

2 English muffins, split and toasted
canned marinara spaghetti sauce
4 slices Mozzarella cheese
½ teaspoon oregano

Spread the muffin halves generously with marinara sauce, cover each with a slice of Mozzarella, and sprinkle with oregano.

Slide under the broiler and cook until cheese melts.

2 SERVINGS

Eggs and Darts

6 hard-cooked eggs, shelled and cut in half lengthwise
2 tablespoons melted butter
2 tablespoons grated Parmesan cheese
1 teaspoon salt
½ teaspoon dry mustard
few grains cayenne (more if you like it hot)
12 anchovy fillets

Remove the egg yolks and mash, adding the cheese and seasonings. Blend well, taste for seasoning, and stuff back into the whites. Lay a dart (anchovy, to you) across each.

Chick-Peas Marshall

½ pound chick-peas, soaked overnight
2 tablespoons cracked wheat, soaked 2 hours
2 cloves garlic
1 teaspoon cumin seed
1 teaspoon salt
2 tablespoons flour
dash coriander
dash chili powder
fat for frying

Mix all the ingredients and grind in a mortar or meat grinder, or put into a blender until mealy.

Form into small balls, and fry in hot fat until golden brown. Serve with martinis.

Huygens Pâté

½ pound chicken livers
4 tablespoons minced onion
¼ teaspoon thyme
½ cup chicken bouillon
1 clove garlic, minced
¼ cup butter, softened
¼ teaspoon dry mustard
½ cup cracker crumbs
3 slices crisp bacon, crumbled
½ teaspoon pepper

Simmer the livers, onion, and thyme in the bouillon 15 minutes. Cool.

Put the cooked livers, ¼ of the broth, and the remaining ingredients into a blender, and blend at low speed; then beat at high speed until creamy and smooth.

Remove to a chilled platter and form into a brick. Refrigerate 2 hours and serve sliced.

8 SERVINGS

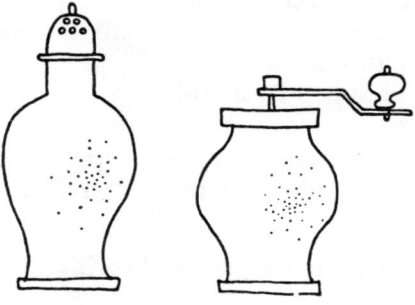

Suburban Spread

2 very ripe avocados
2 medium-sized tomatoes, finely chopped
1 onion, minced
Salsa Jalapeña
lemon juice
salt

Mash avocados with a fork and mix in the remaining ingredients. Use plenty of salt, but watch the hot Jalapeñas. Spread on crackers or tortilla chips and serve immediately, or place in an airtight container to prevent darkening.

Heroes Saarinen

1 long loaf French bread
soft butter
½ pound sliced boiled ham
½ pound sliced smoked salmon
several lettuce leaves, dipped in a mixture of 3 parts oil and 1 part vinegar
2 teaspoons chopped fresh dill

Slice the French bread lengthwise, spread bottom half with butter, and lay on the ham and salmon slices.

Cover with the lettuce leaves and sprinkle with dill.

Cover with top half of the bread, cut diagonally into small slices. Secure with toothpicks and serve with cocktails.

6 TO 8 SERVINGS

Soups and Stews

"Whoever thought of reducing taxes on buildings that spent ½ of 1% on fine art certainly didn't think it through!"

Bauhaus Chowder

2 dozen chowder clams, scrubbed
1 quart water
1 stalk celery, diced
1 onion, diced
1 clove garlic, minced
½ bay leaf
1 sprig parsley
½ cup potatoes, peeled and diced
1 ounce salt pork, diced
½ onion, minced
½ stalk celery, finely chopped
½ leek (white part only), finely chopped
1 tablespoon flour
½ cup light cream, warmed
1 tablespoon butter
minced parsley

Put the clams into a large pot with a quart of cold water. Add the celery, onion, garlic, bay leaf, and parsley. Cover the pot and simmer for 10 minutes.

Remove the clams (discarding the shells), mince them, and set aside.

Remove the stock, strain thoroughly, and return to the pot. Add the potatoes and simmer for 15 minutes or until potatoes are tender.

Meanwhile, in a second pot, render the pork, add the onion, celery, and leek, and sprinkle with flour. Cook for 5 minutes longer, then stir in the hot stock and simmer for 10 minutes.

Stir in the minced clams, cream, and butter.

Serve garnished with minced parsley.

4 SERVINGS

Emery Broth

1 tablespoon butter
2 tablespoons flour
1 tablespoon sugar
2 bottles beer
juice of ½ lemon
lemon peel, chopped
½ teaspoon (or 1 stick) cinnamon
1 pint hot milk
2 eggs
salt and pepper
rye toast

In a saucepan brown the flour and sugar in melted butter.

Add the beer, lemon juice, chopped lemon peel, and cinnamon, and simmer a few minutes.

Add the hot milk in which the eggs have been beaten, season to taste, and serve with toasted rye bread.

4 SERVINGS

Consommaybeck

2 cans consommé
2 cans chicken broth
2 tablespoons cooked peas
1 tablespoon cooked string beans
¼ cup julienned cooked carrots
¼ cup julienned cooked leeks
1 teaspoon salt
½ teaspoon freshly ground pepper
1 teaspoon sherry

Mix all the ingredients together, heat and serve.

4 SERVINGS

Soups and Stews

Curry Chandigarh

1 tart apple, peeled and chopped
1 small onion, chopped
4 cups consommé
1 cup cream
1 teaspoon salt
½ teaspoon pepper
curry powder

Simmer the apple, onion, and consommé 15 minutes. Strain and add the cream, salt and pepper, and curry to taste.

Serve hot or cold.

6 SERVINGS

Post and Lentil Soup

½ pound lentils, soaked overnight
salt
2 tablespoons butter
2 tablespoons flour
2 strips cooked bacon or sliced frankfurters or other sausage
a little vinegar
croutons

Cook the lentils in 2 quarts salted water about an hour or until soft.

In a small skillet melt the butter, stir in the flour and about a cup of the lentil water until smooth.

Add this thickener, the meat, and vinegar to soup. Heat, stir, and serve with croutons.

4-6 SERVINGS

Minestrone Michelangelo

1 cup dried white beans, soaked overnight
1 quart water
⅛ pound salt pork, cubed
1 onion, finely chopped
1 clove garlic (or less, if you want)
1 can tomato paste
2 cups hot consommé
1 cup chopped cabbage
1 cup elbow marcaroni
salt and pepper
grated Parmesan cheese

Simmer the beans in the water until almost tender.

Add the salt pork, onion, garlic, tomato paste, and consommé. Simmer 20 minutes longer.

Add the cabbage. Simmer 15 minutes longer.

Add the macaroni, season to taste, and simmer 10 minutes longer.

Add additional water if needed—soup should be thick.

Serve with grated cheese on top.

8 SERVINGS

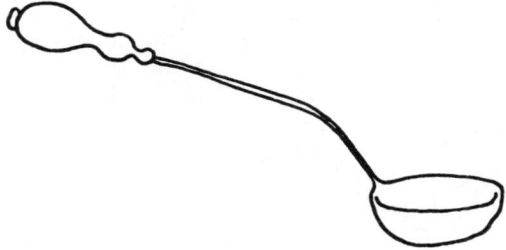

No Risk Bisque

2 tablespoons cubed salt pork
2 tablespoons chopped onion
1 tablespoon butter
2 tablespoons flour
½ teaspoon paprika
½ teaspoon salt
1 teaspoon Worcestershire
dash tabasco
½ cup clam broth
2 teaspoons lemon juice
1 cup chopped clams (fresh or canned)
4 cups milk

Sauté the salt pork in a saucepan until crisp. Add the chopped onion and continue cooking until not quite soft. Stir in the flour and cook 3 or 4 minutes.

Add the paprika, salt Worcestershire, tabasco, clam broth, and lemon juice. Cook, stirring, about 2 minutes.

Reduce the heat, add the clams, and milk, and heat almost to the boiling point.

4 SERVINGS

Eclectic Stew

½ cup wine vinegar
½ cup water
1 cup red wine
1 onion, sliced
1 teaspoon dry mustard
2 whole cloves
1 teaspoon freshly ground pepper
2 teaspoons salt
1 bay leaf
1 package frozen rabbit (about 2 pounds)
4 tablespoons flour
4 tablespoons butter
½ tablespoon sugar
½ cup sour cream
flour

Make a marinade by mixing the first nine ingredients together.

Defrost the rabbit, cut it into serving pieces, cover it with the marinade, and refrigerate 24 hours.

Remove the rabbit pieces, dry well, dust with flour, and brown in the butter, using a heavy skillet.

Add 1 cup of the marinade (strained), cover, and stew about 1-½ hours or until tender.

Remove the rabbit to a heated platter, stir the sugar and sour cream into the sauce, thicken with flour if necessary, check the seasoning, pour over the rabbit and serve.

4 SERVINGS

Cloister Stew

2 tablespoons butter
1 teaspoon Worcestershire sauce
1 teaspoon paprika
½ teaspoon pepper
½ teaspoon celery salt
1 dozen medium-sized oysters
oyster liquor
1 pint milk, half-and-half, or cream, as desired
butter
paprika

Get the top of a double boiler as hot as possible without letting the top pan touch the water in the bottom pan. Put in the butter, Worcestershire, paprika, pepper, and celery salt.

Stir in the oysters, let them froth for half a minute, then pour in the liquor and boil hard for half a minute longer.

Add the milk, half-and-half, or cream, bring to the boiling point, pour into bowls, add a pat of butter, a dash of paprika, and serve.

2 SERVINGS

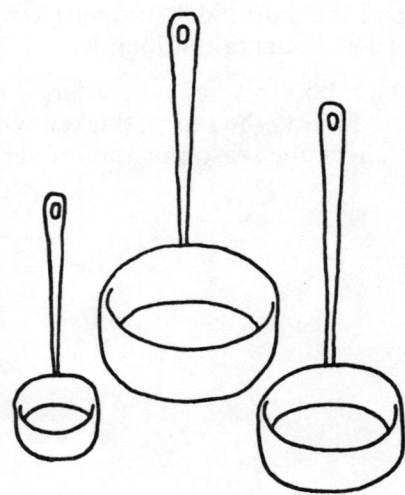

F.W. Dodgepodge

2 medium onions, chopped
2 green peppers, diced
2 tomatoes, chopped
2 tablespoons oil
1 tablespoon paprika
little salt
4 potatoes, peeled and diced
2 cups water
1 pound frankfurters, cut into ½-inch slices
cayenne

Sauté the onion, peppers, and tomatoes in the oil until soft, using a medium pot.

Stir in the paprika and salt, add the potatoes and water, and simmer about 15 minutes or until potatoes are cooked.

Add the frankfurters, cook 15 minutes longer, sprinkle with cayenne and serve in bowls.

4 SERVINGS

Stew Newell Jacobsen

1 pint bay scallops (or sea scallops, cut in half)
1 tablespoon butter
2 cups half-and-half, or 1 cup each of milk and cream
salt
pepper
butter

Using a heavy saucepan, sauté the scallops in the butter 5 minutes.

Add the milk and seasonings, and cook over low heat 15 minutes. Add a dab of butter, and serve.

4 SERVINGS

Pot Luckman

½ pound brisket of beef, cut up
½ pound shin of beef, cut up
¼ pound salt pork, diced
1 onion
1 clove garlic
1 carrot
1 teaspoon salt
pinch rosemary
water
2 medium onions
2 small carrots
1 turnip, quartered
2 potatoes, peeled and quartered
2 pieces marrow bone
freshly ground peper

Put the brisket, shin, pork, onion, garlic, carrot, salt, and rosemary into a pot. Pour in enough water to cover and boil rapidly 10 minutes. Skim.

Reduce heat, cover, and simmer an hour.

Add the onions, carrots, turnip, potatoes, and marrow bones. Cover and simmer 1 hour longer or until vegetables are tender.

Serve in bowls sprinkled with freshly ground pepper.

4 TO 6 SERVINGS

Mullion Stew

2 pounds mutton or lamb, cut into cubes
2 tablespoons flour
1 tablespoon curry powder
1 teaspoon salt
2 onions, sliced
2 carrots, sliced
2 apples, peeled and sliced
1 small turnip, sliced
1 *bouquet garni* (parsley, thyme, bay leaf)
1 pint hot water
the juice of ½ lemon
salt and pepper

Remove the fat from the meat and melt it in a large, heavy saucepan or pot.

Dredge the meat in a mixture of the flour, curry, and salt, and brown it lightly in the fat.

Toss in the vegetables and apples, and any of the flour mixture that might be left, and cook for 15 minutes.

Add the *bouquet garni*, pour in the hot water, cover and cook for 3 hours. Skim the scum and excess fat that rises to the top.

Add the lemon juice, season, and simmer a few minutes.

6 SERVINGS

Shrimp Jamb Alaya

2 onions, chopped
2 tablespoons lard
2 tablespoons flour
1 cup chopped tomatoes
1 cup chopped green pepper
1 cup chopped ham
3 cups shelled raw shrimp
1 clove garlic, minced
1 teaspoon salt
½ teaspoon pepper
¼ teaspoon cayenne
1 cup uncooked rice
3 cups boiling water

In a heavy pot, sauté the onions in the lard, sift in the flour, stirring. Add the tomattoes, peppers, ham, shrimp, and seasonings. Cook and stir 10 minutes.

Add the rice and boiling water. Close the pot tightly and cook over low heat until rice is cooked.

6 SERVINGS

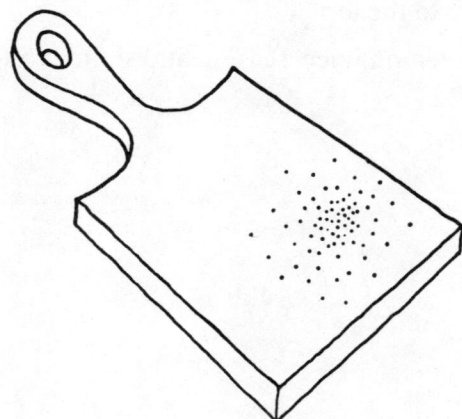

Eggs, Cheeses, and Pasta

"Do you know the heat loss in this house would fry 896,342 eggs?"

Von Eckardt Boiled Eggs

6 hard-boiled eggs, shelled and halved
½ cup Cheddar cheese, cubed
1 cup evaporated milk
1 teaspoon salt
½ teaspoon dry mustard
¼ teaspoon curry powder
1 cup bread crumbs
2 tablespoons butter
buttered toast

Preheat oven to 350 degrees.

Put the cheese and milk into a saucepan and cook over low heat. Add the salt, mustard, and curry. Stir until smooth and creamy.

Put the eggs into a baking dish, cover with the cheese sauce, top with bread crumbs, and dot with butter.

Bake until brown and serve on toast.

4 SERVINGS

Safdie Boiled Eggs

Put the eggs into a saucepan and cover with cold water. Bring slowly to the boiling point. For very soft eggs, remove immediately; for soft eggs, simmer 2 minutes; for medium eggs, simmer 3 to 5 minutes; for hard-cooked eggs, simmer 12 to 15 minutes.

Eggers Benedict

2 tablespoons flour
2 tablespoons melted butter
1 cup milk
salt and pepper
2 egg yolks
6 tablespoons melted butter
1 tablespoon lemon juice

Over low heat, stir the flour into 2 tablespoons melted butter. Add the milk and, using a wire whisk, blend until smooth. Stir in the egg yolks, 6 tablespoons melted butter, and the lemon juice. Set aside and keep warm.

4 eggs, poached
2 English muffins, split and toasted
4 thin slices ham, sautéed 5 minutes

Place a slice of ham on each of the muffin halves, top with a poached egg, and spoon on the sauce.

2 SERVINGS

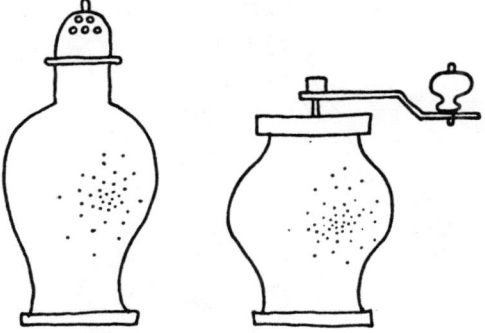

Eggs, Cheeses and Pasta

SOMelette Parmentier

4 eggs, beaten slightly
4 tablespoons water
½ teaspoon salt
⅛ teaspoon pepper
2 tablespoons butter
1 ½ cup finely diced cooked potatoes, sautéed in butter

Mix together the eggs, water, and seasonings and set aside.

Melt the butter in a hot omelet pan and, when it begins to sizzle, pour in the egg mixture and turn down the heat a little.

As the omelet cooks, lift it with a spatula so that the uncooked parts may run under. Continue until the whole is creamy. Spoon in the cooked potatoes, fold double, and turn out onto a warm platter.

2 SERVINGS

Ham and Aecks

2 slices ham ¼-inch thick
1 tablespoon butter
4 eggs

Put the ham into a hot, heavy skillet, and cook on both sides. Remove to heated plates.

Fry the eggs in the same skillet, adding butter if needed. Cover and cook slowly until whites are solid. Serve with the ham.

2 SERVINGS

Parthen on Toast

2 tablespoons butter
2 tablespoons flour
¼ teaspoon dry mustard
¼ teaspoon salt
2 cups milk
¾ cup diced cooked ham
3 hard-cooked eggs, quartered
4 slices toast

Heat the butter in a saucepan, stir in the flour and seasonings. Cook slowly until smooth and creamy. Remove from heat and stir in the milk. Heat again stirring constantly.
Add the ham and eggs. Stir until heated throughout, working carefully so as not to break up the eggs. Serve on toast.

4 SERVINGS

Rabbit Adam

½ pound Cheddar- or Cheshire-type cheese, cut small
2 tablespoons butter
½ teaspoon salt
½ teaspoon dry mustard
few grains cayenne
dash Worcestershire sauce
½ cup beer or ale
1 egg slightly beaten
4 slices toast

Put the cheese, butter, and seasonings into a double boiler or chafing dish over low heat, and cook-stir until cheese melts.

Add the beer and egg, stirring until thick. Check seasoning and serve on toast.

4 SERVINGS

Fondue Ledoux

¾ cup dry white wine
1 pound aged Swiss cheese, diced
salt
pepper
nutmeg
2 tablespoons kirsch

Rub a fondue pot, chafing dish, or heavy casserole with cut garlic; pour in wine and heat over very low heat until bubbly.

Add the cheese, cook-stir until melted and smooth. Season to taste and stir in the kirsch.

Dip crusty chunks of French bread into the fondue and enjoy.

4 SERVINGS

Cheese Soufflot

4 tablesppons butter
4 tablespoons flour
1 cup milk
½ teaspoon salt
few grains cayenne
1 cup grated cheese (Cheddar, Swiss, Parmesan, blue, or a combination)
4 egg yolks, beaten until light
4 egg whites, beaten until stiff

Preheat oven to 325 degrees.

Melt the butter over low heat, stir in the flour; gradually add the milk, blending with a wire whisk until thick and smooth. Season with salt and cayenne and stir in the cheese until smooth.

Remove mixture from the heat, add the egg yolks. Cool. Stir in a tablespoon of the egg white, then fold in the rest.

Transfer to an unbuttered 1½-quart baking dish with straight sides. Set the dish into a pan of hot water and bake 30 to 35 minutes. (For a French-style creamy soufflé, bake only 25 minutes.)

Serve immediately.

4 SERVINGS

Quiche Stone

1 cup flour
1 egg yolk, lightly beaten
½ cup butter, softened
2 tablespoons water
pinch salt
½ pound sliced bacon, fried crisp and crumbled
1½ cups grated or diced Gruyère cheese
4 eggs
2 cups heavy cream
½ teaspoon salt
¼ teaspoon dry mustard
dash nutmeg
dash cayenne

Preheat oven to 400 degrees.

Make a soft pastry dough by beating together the flour, egg yolk, butter, water, and salt. Chill for half an hour, and roll out on a floured board into a thin pastry shell. Place in a 9-inch pie pan and trim the edges. Cover with wax paper, and bake 10 minutes.

Sprinkle the bacon and cheese bits onto the pie shell. Lightly beat the eggs with the cream and seasonings, and pour into the shell.

Reduce the oven temperature to 325 degrees, and bake the quiche until golden and the center is firm.

Cut into 12 slices for canapés or 6 for a luncheon dish.

Melange Moholy-Nagy

2 cups elbow macaroni, cooked
2 tablespoons grated onion
3 cups shredded Cheddar cheese
1 teaspoon salt
½ teaspoon pepper
2 cups McKim, Mead and White sauce (see page 98)
1 tablespoon butter

Preheat oven to 375 degrees.

Put half the macaroni into a 2-quart casserole, sprinkle with half the onion, cheese, salt, and pepper.

Repeat, then pour the white sauce over all and dot with butter. Cover.

Bake 30 minutes, then uncover and bake 15 minutes longer.

6 SERVINGS

Nervi Noodles

½ pound broad egg noodles
¼ pound soft unsalted butter
¼ teaspoon salt
Freshly ground pepper
¼ pound grated Parmesan cheese

Drop the noodles into a pot of salted boiling water and cook until barely tender (*al dente*).

Drain and transfer to a heated dish. Add the butter and turn over and over with a large fork and spoon until noodles are well coated with the butter.

Add the seasonings and cheese and continue to turn until cheese is melted.

4 SERVINGS

Linguine Bernini

½ pound linguine
4 tablespoons olive oil
2 cloves garlic, minced
1½ cups minced clams
½ cup clam juice
½ cup dry white wine
½ teaspoon pepper
¼ cup chopped parsley

Cook the linguine until just tender in boiling salted water. Drain and remove to a heated platter. Keep warm.

Heat the oil, and sauté the garlic in it for 2 minutes. Add the remaining ingredients, and simmer about 10 minutes.

Pour the sauce over the linguine, mix, and serve.
4 TO 6 SERVINGS

Noodles Romanesque

8 ounces broad noodles
2 tablespoons softened butter
2 cups sour cream
½ cup grated Parmesan cheese
1 tablespoon chopped chives
1 clove garlic, minced
1 teaspoon salt
¼ teaspoon pepper

Cook the noodles in salted boling water until softened. Drain, and stir in the butter.

Mix together the sour cream, ¼ cup of Parmesan cheese, the chives, garlic, and seasonings.

Blend the buttered noodles and sour cream mixture, sprinkle with remaining cheese, and serve.
6 TO 8 SERVINGS

Rossetti Spaghetti

1 package (8 ounces) spaghetti
salt
6 slices bacon
1 egg
1 tablespoon cream
Parmesan cheese

Heat to boiling a large pot of salted water (1 teaspoon of salt per quart of water). Stand the spaghetti on end in the water (do not break up) and cook and stir 12 to 15 minutes until just tender (*al dente*). Drain.

In a large heavy skillet, fry the bacon until crisp. Crumble, return to the skillet along with the spaghetti, and cook, tossing, for a minute or so.

Beat the egg with the cream, pour over the spaghetti, and cook, stirring, a minute longer. Serve at once, topped with Parmesan cheese.

4 to 5 SERVINGS

Eternal Ziti

1 ½-pound package Roman ziti
1 tablespoon salt
¼ pound butter, softened
2 cups tomato sauce
2 cups grated Parmesan cheese

Boil the ziti in salted water until just tender—do not overcook.

Drain and put on a heated platter, add the butter, tomato sauce, and half of the Parmesan cheese. Toss to mix thoroughly, and serve topped with the remaining cheese.

4 to 6 SERVINGS

Paestum Pasta

1 package (8 onces) spaghetti
salt
¼ cup olive oil
2 cloves garlic, split
6 anchovies, cut up
grated Parmesan cheese

Heat to boiling a large pot of salted water (1 teaspoon of salt per quart of water). Stand the spaghetti on end in the water and cook and stir 12 to 15 minutes until just tender (*al dente*).

Drain, put on a heated platter, and keep warm.

Heat the oil with the garlic a few minutes, remove and discard the garlic, and add the anchovies.

Pour this sauce over the spaghetti, sprinkle generously with Parmesan cheese, and toss until well mixed.

4 TO 5 SERVINGS

Meats

"If you can't stand the heat, get out of the Open Plan!"

Las Vegas Strip Steak

2½ pounds porterhouse steak with tenderloin, tail, and bone removed
1 clove garlic, cut
salt
freshly ground pepper
1 tablespoon butter
chopped parsley

Set oven regulator for broiling.

Trim excess fat from steak, slash edges of remaining fat, and rub thoroughly with cut side of garlic.

Place on oiled rack of broiler pan about 2 inches from heat.

Broil until top side is deep brown (steak should be about half done at this stage).

Season top side with salt and pepper.

Turn and brown other side (cut small incision to determine doneness).

Remove to heated carving board or platter, place butter beneath, season with salt and pepper, and garnish with parsley. A1A sauce may be served on the side.

4 SERVINGS

Filet Boullée

2½ pounds filets mignons, cut into 4 (½-inch thick)
    slices of equal size
1 (1-ounce) can pâté de foie gras
2 tablespoons melted butter
freshly ground pepper
salt
chopped water cress

With a sharp knife cut deep slashes into sides of filets.

Insert pâté de foie gras into these pockets.

Brush generously with melted butter and sprinkle with a little pepper.

Broil in a heavy skillet at high heat, season with salt, and serve garnished with chopped water cress.

4 SERVINGS

Williamsburgers

1 pound ground round steak
salt
freshly ground pepper
4 slices Smithfield ham
4 rolls, heated or toasted

Form the ground steak into 8 flat patties and pan broil on both sides to desired doneness.

Season to taste, place 2 patties on the bottom half of a sliced roll, insert a slice of ham between the patties, and cover with the top half of the roll.

4 SERVINGS

Theo van Doesburgers

1 pound ground round steak
1 teaspoon salt
1 teaspoon pepper
1 teaspoon Worcestershire
4 slices American cheese
4 heated rolls

Season the hamburger, knead in the Worcestershire, and form into 4 patties.

Place each onto the bottom slice of a roll, and broil 3 minutes.

Cover each with a slice of cheese and continue cooking until cheese melts.

Cover with the top halves of the rolls and toast a minute or so.

Modulor Meatloaf with A1A Sauce

¾ pound ground beef
¼ pound ground lean pork
¼ pound ground veal
¾ cup dry bread crumbs
1 egg, beaten
¼ cup finely chopped onion
salt and pepper
½ teaspoon dry mustard
2 tablespoons A1A sauce

Preheat oven to 350 degrees.

Mix together all the ingredients except the A1A sauce, form into a loaf and place into a greased baking pan.

Brush the A1A sauce over all and bake for 1½ hours.

4 SERVINGS

Porter House Steak

2½ pounds porterhouse steak
¾ pound large mushrooms, peeled and with stems removed
1 tablespoon butter
salt
dash nutmeg
2 tablespoons cream
freshly ground pepper

Trim excess fat from steak, and pan-broil in a heavy skillet over high heat to desired doneness.

Remove to a hot platter.

Add the butter, salt, and nutmeg to the pan juices. Select 4 large mushroom caps and chop the rest. Sauté all for a few minutes until golden.

Remove the 4 mushroom caps and place on the steak.

Add cream to the skillet, simmer, stirring, for a few minutes, and pour over the steak. Sprinkle lavishly with pepper.

4 SERVINGS

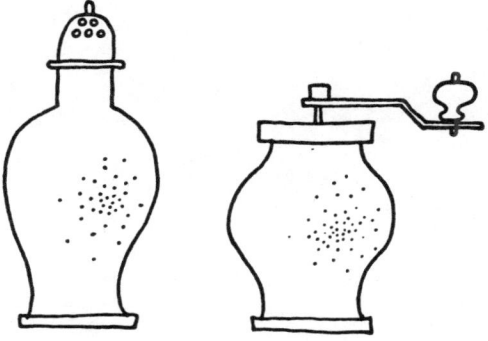

Roast Beef au Joist

2- to 4- rib roast of beef, with short ribs removed
flour
freshly ground pepper
salt

Preheat oven to 500 degrees.
Keep meat at room temperature for 2½ hours before cooking. Place into an open shallow pan, fat side up, and sprinkle with a little flour and season with salt and freshly ground pepper.

Slide into the oven and cook 15 minutes per rib.

Turn off the oven. Allow roast to remain in the oven without opening the door until oven is lukewarm, or about 2 hours.

Roast will be done—crunchy brown on the outside and having an internal heat that will be suitable for serving for as long as 4 hours.

Remove roast to a heated platter, and put pan on top stove. Heat ans scrape, adding a little water. Boil up. Pour juice into a gravy boat and serve with the roast.

2 SERVINGS PER RIB

Carrère Roast Beef with Hastings Pudding

4 to 6 pounds of boneless rib roast
1 cup flour
½ teaspoon salt
1 cup milk
2 eggs

Preheat oven to 325 degrees.

Place meat fat side up on rack in a shallow roasting pan. Insert meat thermometer so that tip is in thickest part of the beef.

Roast until thermometer shows 140 degrees for rare beef. Remove from oven and keep warm.

Spoon ½ cup of the drippings into a square pan, increase oven temperature to 425 degrees.

Mix together the flour, salt, milk, and eggs with a rotary hand beater, and pour into the pan of drippings. Bake 20 minutes and serve with the roast.

8 TO 10 SERVINGS

Chili Kahn Carne

3 tablespoons olive oil
2 cloves garlic, crushed
1 large onion, chopped
2 pounds beef, cubed or chopped
10 dried chilies
3 tablespoons chili powder
1 teaspoon oregano
1 teaspoon cumin seed, crushed
1 teaspoon salt
2 cups beef bouillon

In a large heavy skillet, sauté the garlic and onions in olive oil for a couple of minutes, throw in the meat, and brown.

Remove the stems, seeds, and skins from the chilies. (Boiling them for about 15 minutes will make this easier).

Add the chili powder, oregano, ground cumin seed, and salt to the meat. Pour in the bouillon and cook until the meat is tender and the flavors are well blended.

You serve this chile in a bowl with Mexican pink beans that have been soaked overnight and boiled until tender, or with canned kidney beans diluted with a little water. Control the spiciness by using more (or less) of the liquid from the bean pot.

Vary the dish by adding a cup of canned tomatoes and/or a minced green pepper. You can put in a little celery seed, cayenne, bay leaf, basil, or almost anything your heartburn desires.

It is hard to cook chili too long. It is even better reheated the next day.

8 SERVINGS

Schinkel Sauerbraten

3 pounds boned beef, chuck or round
3 cups beer
2 cups water
1 onion, sliced
1 tomato, chopped
1 lemon, sliced
1 bay leaf
2 whole cloves
4 pepper corns
3 tablespoons flour
3 tablespoons oil
1 lemon, sliced
1 tablespoon sugar
1 teaspoon salt
½ cup sour cream

In a large bowl or enamel pot, mix together the beer, water, onion, tomato, lemon, and seasonings. Put the beef into this marinade, cover, and refrigerate 2 or 3 days, turning several times.

Remove the meat, pat dry, and dredge with flour. Strain the marinade and reserve.

Brown the meat on all sides, add 1½ cups of the strained marinade, the sliced lemon, the sugar and salt, cover, and cook over low heat 2½ to 3 hours, or until meat is very tender. Add more liquid if necessary.

Remove meat to a heated platter and slice. Skim the fat from the sauce, strain, and stir in the sour cream. Heat and serve over the sliced meat.

8 SERVINGS

Gropius TACos with Quonset Hot Sauce

1 tablespoon oil
1 medium onion, chopped
¾ pound lean ground beef
½ green pepper, chopped
1 tomato, peeled and chopped
1 clove garlic, minced
½ teaspoon oregano
½ teaspoon vinegar
1 teaspoon salt
shredded lettuce
8 tortillas
Quonset Hot Sauce (see page 95)

Sauté the onion and meat in the oil, using a heavy skillet. Add the tomato, garlic, and seasonings and cook 15 minutes.

Preheat oven to 350 degrees.

Warm the tortillas in the oven to soften, and spread the meat mixture in each. Roll or fold, place seam side down, into a baking dish, and cook to desired crispness.

Serve with shredded lettuce and Quonset Hot Sauce.

4 SERVINGS

Franks Lloyd Wright

1 onion, chopped
½ cup celery, chopped
½ green pepper, chopped
1 tablespoon bacon fat or butter
1 pound frankfurters, cut in ½-inch pieces
1 large can tomatoes
pinch thyme
pinch oregano
4 slices toast
½ pound Cheddar cheese, diced
¾ cup milk
dash Worcestershire

In a heavy skillet simmer the onion, celery and pepper in oil 10 minutes.

Add the frankfurters, tomatoes, and seasonings and simmer 10 minutes longer.

Spoon the mixture into 4 slices toast, set aside and keep warm.

Heat the cheese, milk, and Worcestershire over low heat until cheese is melted. Spoon over frankfurters and serve.

4 SERVINGS

Knockwurst Knossos

1 onion, diced
1-pound package sauerkraut, washed and drained
2 tablespoons oil
3 knockwursts, cut into 1-inch-thick slices

Put the onion in a large pot with the oil, and sauté until soft.

Add the sauerkraut and knockwurst and cook slowly over low heat at least half an hour, stirring from time to time to prevent burning.

4 SERVINGS

Flying Buttress of Pork with Spice/Thyme

1 2- to 4-pound fresh boned pork butt
1 tablespoon dry mustard
½ teaspoon thyme mixed with ½ teaspoon caraway seed
1 teaspoon salt
1 teaspoon paprika

Preheat oven to 350 degrees.

Mix together the Spice/Thyme seasonings, and rub into the butt.

Place on a rack in a shallow pan and roast uncovered until well done, allowing 45 minutes per pound.

Place onto a heated platter and serve in thin slices.

4 TO 6 SERVINGS

Smith, Hinchman Mixed Gryll

4 lamb chops, 1 inch thick
4 lamb kidneys, split and skewered open
8 small pork sausages, parboiled
4 tomato halves
salt
pepper

Preheat the broiler. Oil the rack, and grill the mixed meats about 5 minutes; turn the chops, add the tomatoes, and grill 5 minutes longer or until chops and tomatoes are done.

Season with salt and pepper.

4 SERVINGS

Meats

Chow Main Street

2 cups julienned lean cooked pork
¼ cup peanut oil
1 cup sliced celery
½ cup chopped onion
3 tablespoons soy sauce
2 cups beef bouillon
1 teaspoon monosodium glutamate
2 tablespoons cornstarch mixed with ½ cup water
1 can sliced mushrooms, drained
1 can fried noodles

In a heavy skillet heat the pork in hot peanut oil. Stir in the celery, onion, soy sauce, bouillon and monosodium glutamate. Cover and simmer half an hour.

Stir in the cornstarch mixture, mushrooms and vegetables. Cook-stir a minute or so and serve over fried noodles.

4 SERVINGS

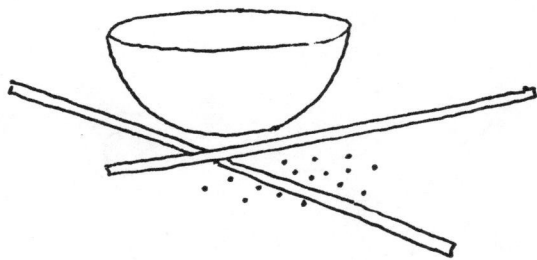

Central Pork Olmsted

4 to 5 pounds loin of pork, center cut (with backbone separated from ribs, and bones sawed through)
6 small potatoes, peeled
4 tart apples, cored and cut into ½-inch slices
brown sugar
flour

Preheat oven to 350 degrees.

Place the pork, fat side up, in a shallow roasting pan, surround with the potatoes, and cook 35 minutes per pound or until meat is fork tender.

Meanwhile, transfer some of the fat from the roasting pan to a skillet and sauté the apple rings until just barely tender, turning once. Sprinkle with brown sugar, cover, and cook until sugar melts.

When roast is done, transfer to a heated platter, surround with potatoes and apple rings, and serve with gravy on the side. (To make gravy, pour off most of the fat from the roasting pan and stir in a little flour, scraping the brown bits from the pan. Cook a few minutes, then stir in water, season to taste, and pour into a gravy boat.)

4 TO 6 SERVINGS

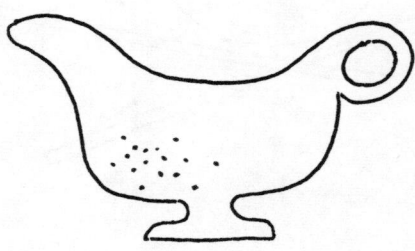

Vaulted Ribs with Bar-O-Que Sauce

4 pounds fresh pork spareribs, 2 rib pieces
salt
pepper
1 lemon, cut
½ cup minced onion
Bar-O-Que Sauce (see page 98)

Preheat oven to 350 degrees.

Arrange the ribs in a shallow baking pan. Season with salt and pepper. Pour a dab of minced onion and a squeeze of lemon juice on each pair of ribs and bake 1½ hours, basting several times with Bar-O-Que Sauce.

4 SERVINGS

Prefab Casserole

1 cup cooked ham, chicken, veal, or fish
2 hard-boiled eggs, chopped
2 cups McKim, Mead and White Sauce (see page 98)
1 cup cooked sliced potatoes
1 cup cooked peas
1 cup buttered bread crumbs

Preheat oven to 375 degrees.

Butter a casserole and sprinkle with some of the bread crumbs. Put in half of each of the remaining ingredients in layers, then repeat with the other half. Top with the remaining bread crumbs.

Bake until crumbs are brown.

6 SERVINGS

Ham HOK with Black-Eyed Peas

2 cups dried black-eyed peas, soaked overnight
4 cured ham hocks, washed
1 medium onion, chopped
1 bay leaf
1 stalk celery, diced
1 clove garlic, minced
1 package frozen okra, thawed
1 teaspoon salt
¼ teaspoon cayenne

Put the hocks in a large pot. Add enough cold water to cover, and simmer over low heat until tender.

Remove the hocks, discard the skin and return the meat to the pot. Drain the peas, and add to the pot with the remaining ingredients (except the okra). Simmer 45 minutes or until peas are tender and liquid is almost absorbed.

Put the okra on top of the peas but do not stir. Cover and cook 15 minutes or until okra is tender.

6 SERVINGS

Moore Pork Sausages with Potatoes

12 sausages
3 tablespoons flour
4 cups hot mashed potatoes

Broil the sausages in a heavy skillet, remove to a bed of mashed potatoes, set aside and keep warm.

Discard all but 2 tablespoons of the juices, and stir in the flour. Gradually add water, stirring until desired thickness is attained. Pour gravy over sausages and mashed potatoes and serve.

4 SERVINGS

Loos Mousse

½ pound ham, finely ground
3 egg whites
½ teaspoon pepper
pinch nutmeg
½ cup heavy cream
grated Parmesan cheese
chopped parsley

Preheat oven to 350 degrees.

In a blender, mix together the ham, egg whites, and seasonings. Stir in the heavy cream, a little at a time.

Fill 4 (or more) buttered individual molds. Set the molds in a pan of hot water, and bake about half an hour, or until firm.

Turn out onto a heated platter, dust with grated cheese, and garnish with parsley.

4 TO 6 SERVINGS

John Nash Hash

4 cups chopped leftover cooked chicken, turkey, or meat
2 tablespoons butter or oil
2 cups chopped boiled potatoes
1 cup chopped onion
1 cup leftover gravy
1 teaspoon salt
½ teaspoon pepper
dash Tabasco

Put all the ingredients into a heavy skillet and cook, stirring, until almost dry.

4 SERVINGS

Meats

Lamb LeMessurier

1 leg lamb, about 6 pounds, with the bone removed and the meat tied up firmly
1 clove garlic, slivered
2 teaspoons salt
1 teaspoon rosemary
Bar-O-Que sauce (see page 98)

Wipe the lamb dry, make several shallow cuts in it, and insert slivers of garlic. Rub with salt and rosemary.

Put the lamb over white-hot charcoals or on a spit in a rotisserie, and cook to desired doneness

Serve with Bar-O-Que sauce.

8 TO 10 SERVINGS

Broiled Lamb Cheops with Pediment Jelly

4 loin lamb chops, 1 inch thick
salt
pepper
Pediment jelly

Preheat oven broiler 10 minutes.

Place the chops on a greased broiler rack and cook 2 inches from the heat for 12 minutes (15 minutes for well-done chops).

Serve with Pediment jelly on the side.

4 SERVINGS

Baked Hughes with Herbs Smith

4 pounds breast of ewe, or lamb
Herbs Smith (2 teaspoons dill, ½ teaspoon rosemary,
    1 teaspoon salt, ½ teaspoon freshly ground pepper)

Preheat oven to 350 degrees.

Place the lamb breast in a shallow baking pan, meaty side up.

Sprinkle with Herbs Smith, and bake uncovered for 1½ hours, or until tender and crisp. Baste from time to time.

4 SERVINGS

Leg of Mitchell-Lama

1 leg of lamb, about 6 pounds
1 clove garlic, slivered
caraway seed or thyme

Preheat oven to 325 degrees.

Make 8 or 10 shallow slits in the leg and insert slivers of garlic. Sprinkle with caraway seed or thyme.

Place the roast in a shallow roasting pan and cook 25 minutes per pound for pink lamb, 35 minutes for well-done.

Remove to a heated platter and make the gravy.

8 SERVINGS

Broiled Muntin Chops

4 mutton chops, 1½ to 2 inches thick
salt
freshly ground pepper
butter

Preheat broiler 10 minutes.

Grease the broiling rack, place the chops on the rack, and cook 2 inches from the heat for 10 to 12 minutes on each side. (Mutton chops should be served rare.)

Season with salt and pepper, spoon the pan juices over the chops, dot with butter, and serve.

4 SERVINGS

Vol au Venturi

1 pound veal sweetbreads
1 teaspoon salt
2 teaspoons vinegar
1 cup McKim, Mead and White sauce (page 98)
4 patty shells, warmed

Simmer the sweetbreads 20 minutes in a quart of water containing 1 teaspoon salt and 2 teaspoons vinegar. Plunge into cold water, drain, and remove the membranes and dark tubes. Cut into small pieces.

Put the sweetbreads into the White sauce, heat, and spoon into the patty shells.

4 SERVINGS

Veal Radieuse

1½ pounds veal cutlets, thinly sliced
1 teaspoon salt
½ teaspoon pepper
flour
½ cup olive oil
2 cloves garlic, split

Pound the cutlets until about ¼-inch thick; season with salt and pepper and sprinkle with flour.

Heat the oil with the garlic, and sauté the cutlets over low heat until golden brown on both sides.

4 SERVINGS

Artnou Veau

1½ to 2 pounds veal, thinly sliced
¼ cup flour
2 tablespoons butter
1 small onion, minced
½ clove garlic, minced
¼ green pepper, minced
1 small tomato, peeled and chopped
½ cup water
½ teaspoon salt
1 tablespoon paprika

Wipe the meat slices dry, coat lightly with flour, and sauté 5 minutes in the butter.

Add the onion, garlic, green pepper, and tomato. Sauté 5 minutes longer, then add the water and seasonings.

Cover and cook over low heat for half an hour or until meat is tender. Check seasoning and add more water, if necessary, to make a thin gravy.

4 SERVINGS

Meats

Cantilever and Henry Bacon

8 slices bacon
1 pound liver, calves' or young beef, cut into slices ¼
    to ½ inch thick
salt
pepper
flour

Pan-fry the bacon and drain on a paper towel.

Wipe the liver dry and remove the thin outside skin and the veins. Season with salt and pepper and cook in the bacon fat 5 minutes.

4 SERVINGS

St. Mark's Venison

3 pounds well-hung venison loin, cut into ½-inch
    slices
olive oil
2 tablespoons bacon fat
½ slice onion
2 tablespoons flour
½ teaspoon salt
⅛ teaspoon pepper
1 cup consommé
½ cup chopped boiled chestnuts

Brush the venison slices with oil and sauté 5 minutes on each side in a heavy skillet. Remove to a heated platter.

To the pan add the bacon fat and onion, and cook slowly for a few minutes until brown. Stir in the flour and seasonings, the onion, add the chestnuts, cook 5 minutes longer, and pour over the venison.

4 SERVINGS

Poultry and Seafood

"What's cooking?"

Baltimore Trussed Capon with Hugh Stuffins

1 4-pound capon, dressed
3 cups bread crumbs
1 cup chopped mushrooms, cooked 5 minutes in butter
1 teaspoon chopped chives
1 teaspoon chopped parsley
pinch nutmeg
butter

Preheat oven to 325 degrees.

Mix together the bread crumbs, mushrooms, and seasonings, and stuff into the bird.
Truss as follows: Press the thighs in close to the body and tie to the tail with string. Close the opening laterally with 3 skewers, lace string along the skewers, and tie. Place the wings close to the body and skewer tightly. Draw the neck skin under the back and fasten with a toothpick.

Place the bird, breast side up, onto a rack in a roasting pan and rub skin with butter. Roast about 3 hours or until tender (drumstick will move easily when done). Keep warm while making the gravy.

Pour off the fat into a cup, returning about 4 tablespoons to the pan. Add 1 cup boiling water, heat, scrape, and stir. Season to taste and strain into a gravy boat.

4 SERVINGS

Chicken Itzá

4 breasts of chicken, cooked and with bone removed
1 4-ounce can pimentos, drained and chopped
2 cups light cream (or evaporated milk)
1 cup chopped Swiss cheese
1 teaspoon salt
½ teaspoon pepper
1 teaspoon chopped parsley

Preheat oven to 325 degrees.

Place the breasts into a buttered shallow baking dish.

Mix together the cream, cheese, and seasonings, pour over the breasts, and bake for 15 or 20 minutes, basting occasionally.

Serve on rice or toast, garnished with parsley.

4 SERVINGS

Hagia Sophia Turkey with Ralph Adams Cranberry Sauce

2 pounds turkey breasts
salt
pepper
flour
2 tablespoons butter
1 tablespoon cooking oil
Ralph Adams Cranberry Sauce (see page 96)

Cut the breasts into serving-size pieces, and pound to flatten slightly.

Season with salt and pepper, and roll in flour.

Sauté in a mixture of the butter and oil until golden brown.

Serve with Ralph Adams Cranberry Sauce.

4 SERVINGS

Marcel Broiler

2 small broiling chickens split (or 1 large chicken quartered)
salt
pepper
½ cup orange juice
½ cup salad oil
2 tablespoons grated orange rind
pinch salt
pinch dry mustard
dash paprika
dash Tabasco

Preheat oven to 550 degrees.

Place the chicken parts on a broiler rack skin side down, sprinkle with salt and pepper, and brush well with a mixture made from the remaining ingredients.

Broil 4 inches from the heat for 10 minutes. Turn, brush again with the orange mixture, and cook 10 minutes longer.

Continue turning, brushing, and cooking until crisp and golden, allowing a total time of about an hour.

4 SERVINGS

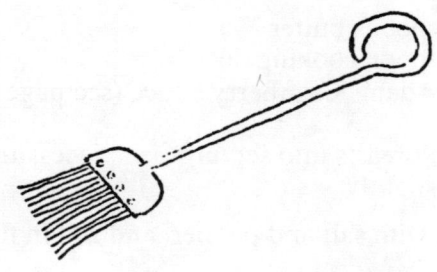

Doric Duck with Carl A. Morse Sauce

1 duck, 4 to 5 pounds, prepared for cooking
salt
paprika
1 1-pound can sauerkraut, rinsed
Carl A. Morse sauce (see page 97)

Preheat oven to 375 degrees.

Wipe the duck dry, and rub inside and out with salt and paprika.

Stuff the sauerkraut into the cavity, and place on a rack in a roasting pan. Sprinkle with paprika. Cook 1½ hours, or until duck is tender. Then remove cover and cook 15 minutes longer at 450 degrees to crisp the skin.

Remove duck to a heated platter and make the Carl A. Morse sauce.

4 SERVINGS

Quail de Stijl

2 quail, plucked and eviscerated
salt
melted butter
buttered toast
watercress

Preheat oven to 350 degrees.

Tie the legs together and fasten close to the body with skewers.
Sprinkle inside with salt. Roast about 15 minutes, or until tender,
basting with butter.

Cut in two down the breast with kitchen shears, and serve cut-side down on toast. Garnish with watercress.

4 SERVINGS

Roman Aque Duck

1 duck, 4 to 5 pounds, prepared for cooking
salt
pepper
4 tablespoons butter
2 oranges, peeled and quartered
½ cup consommé
½ cup dry white wine
1 teaspoon cornstarch

Rub the duck with salt and pepper, brown on all sides in a heavy skillet in the butter.

Scrape white parts from orange skins and cut into strips. Lay across the duck parts. Add the oranges and consommé.

Simmer about 1½ hours or until tender.
Remove duck to a heated platter and keep warm while you make the sauce.

Pour off all but ½ cup of the pan juices, add the wine and bring to the boiling point, stir in the corn starch, add a little water, and stir until thickened. Pour over the duck.

4 SERVINGS

Viollet-le-Duck

1 duck, 4 to 5 pounds, dressed
2 tablespoons vinegar
salt
pepper
paprika
1 large onion, chopped
1 green pepper, chopped
1 tomato, chopped
1 tablespoon cooking oil
1 cup water

Soak the duck for 1 hour in ice water containing the vinegar and 2 tablespoons of salt.

Remove, cut into serving pieces, and season with salt, pepper, and paprika.

Sauté the vegetables in the oil until soft. Do not brown.

Add 1 tablespoon paprika, stir, then add the duck parts and the water.

Simmer, stirring occasionally, for an hour (or more) until duck is tender, adding more water if necessary.

Correct the seasonings and serve.

4 SERVINGS

Cornice Hen

1 Cornish hen, split
1 teaspoon salt
½ teaspoon pepper
1 tablespoon flour
2 tablespoons bacon fat
1 cup cream
cornstarch
2 slices buttered toast

Sprinkle the hen halves with salt, pepper, and flour. Heat bacon fat in a heavy skillet, and brown the hen parts on both sides.

Add the cream, cover, and cook about an hour over very low heat, or until tender.

Place the hen parts on the toast.

Thicken the juices in the skillet by stirring in a little cornstarch. Check the seasoning, and pour sauce over the hen.

2 SERVINGS

Coquilles Ely Jacques Kahn

1 pound bay scallops (or sea scallops cut up)
1 tablespoon butter
2 tablespoons minced onion
juice of ½ lemon
½ teaspoon salt
pinch marjoram
dash paprika
1 cup dry white wine
1½ cups chopped mushrooms
⅓ cup butter
¼ cup flour
1 cup cream
2 teaspoons minced parsley
dry bread crumbs
butter

Melt 1 tablespoon butter in a heavy saucepan, and sauté the onion a few minutes.

Add the scallops, lemon juice, seasonings, and wine. Simmer 10 minutes.

Add the mushrooms, and simmer 2 minutes longer. Drain off the liquid and reserve.

Melt ⅓ cup butter over low heat in a heavy saucepan, stir in the flour and cook until bubbly.

Remove from heat; stir in the cream and reserved liquid, and then the parsley. Cook-stir for a minute or so, then pour over the scallops. Stir.

Spoon the scallops into 6 individual *coquilles* or ramekins. Sprinkle with bread crumbs, dot with butter, and broil 6 or 7 minutes 5 inches away from the broiler.

6 COQUILLES

Bass Gilbert

2 pounds small-mouth, large-mouth, or calico bass
2 teaspoons salt
pepper
½ cup cornmeal, yellow or white
½ cup flour
2 tablespoons butter
2 tablespoons bacon fat
2 teaspoons chopped parsley
1 lemon, sliced

Dress the fish, wipe them dry with a paper towel, and season well with salt and pepper.

Roll them in a mixture of cornmeal and flour until well coated.

Heat the butter and bacon fat in a skillet, and brown the fish for 4 minutes on each side, or until they are golden brown and the flesh flakes when fork-tested.

Serve at once, garnished with chopped parsley and lemon slices.

4 TO 6 SERVINGS

Fish von Erlach

3 pounds fish steak (or steaks)
1 teaspoon salt
¼ cup butter
1 clove garlic, crushed
¼ cup sliced olives (ripe, green, or stuffed)
1 teaspoon paprika
½ teaspoon pepper
2 teaspoons lemon juice
chopped fresh dill

Salt the steak and pan broil it in a heavy skillet, using a little oil if necessary to prevent sticking (test with a fork and remove when fish is flaky—3 minutes on each side should do it). Set aside on a warm platter.

Using the same skillet, melt the butter, add the garlic, olives, paprika, pepper, and lemon juice, and sauté gently for a few minutes.

Pour the sauce over the steak and garnish with chopped fresh dill.

4 SERVINGS

Capital Carp

1 dressed carp (3 to 5 pounds)
2 onions, chopped
½ cup fish stock or clam juice
1 cup Burgundy wine
4 anchovy fillets
2 teaspoons flour creamed with 2 teaspoons butter
1 egg yolk, lightly beaten

Preheat oven to 350 degrees.

Place the onions and then the fish into a greased, foil-lined baking dish, add the stock, Burgundy, and garnish with anchovy fillets.

Bake, uncovered, about half an hour, or until fish flakes easily, basting often with the pan liquid.

Remove the fish to a preheated platter, and strain the liquid.

Place the liquid into a small saucepan, heat, stir in the flour creamed with the butter, and simmer for a minute.

Add a little of the hot liquid to the egg yolk, then stir it into the sauce. Pour over the fish and serve at once.

4 TO 6 SERVINGS

Fish Tishman

1 pound eel and 2 pounds striped bass (or bluefish), cleaned, boned, and cut into 3-inch pieces.
3 pounds lobster, split, cleaned, and with claws cracked
1 onion, sliced
2 cloves garlic, sliced
2 leeks (white parts only), sliced
1 bay leaf
2 teaspoons chopped parsley
2 tablespoons olive oil
3 cups dry white wine
salt and pepper
fish stock or clam juice
few grains saffron, powdered

Put all the ingredients except the stock and saffron into a shallow ovenware glass or stainless-steel dish, and marinate for about 2 hours, stirring from time to time.

Add enough fish stock to cover the fish, add the saffron, cover, and cook at low heat about 15 minutes, or until fish flakes with a fork.

Serve with chunks of French bread.

8 SERVINGS

Lobster Termi Door

4 1¼ pound lobsters, cleaned and cooked
½ cup melted butter
1 cup chopped mushrooms
½ teaspoon salt
½ teaspoon pepper
1 teaspoon English mustard
1 tablespoon Worcestershire sauce
few grains cayenne
½ cup sherry
¼ cup cognac
1½ cups cream
3 egg yolks, beaten until creamy
½ cup bread crumbs
½ cup grated Parmesan cheese
paprika

Preheat oven to 400 degrees.

Remove the meat from the lobsters, and cut in ½-inch pieces. Reserve the shells.

Sauté the mushrooms in half the butter for 10 minutes. Remove from heat, and add the lobster meat, seasonings, sherry, cognac, cream, egg yolks, and bread crumbs. Mix well.

Fill the lobster shells with this mixture, pour on the remaining butter, and dust with Parmesan and paprika.

Place on a baking sheet and bake 10 minutes.

4 SERVINGS

Mies van der Roe

4 small pairs (or 2 large pairs) of fresh shad roe
boiling water
salt
juice of ½ lemon
4 slices bacon
4 lemon slices

Put the roes in a skillet, cover with boiling salted water, and add the lemon juice. Parboil gently for 10 minutes. Remove, drain, and let stand in cold water 5 minutes.

Sauté the bacon in a heavy skillet, remove, and sauté the roes in the bacon fat 10 minutes or until golden.

Serve with lemon slices and bacon.

4 SERVINGS

Finial Haddie in Milk

1 pound finnan haddie, soaked overnight in cold
    water
milk
butter
pepper

Put the finnan haddie in a heavy skillet, cover with milk, and poach gently over low heat for 25 minutes, or until tender.

Remove to a heated platter, dot with butter, and sprinkle with pepper.

4 SERVINGS

Sturgeon Soane

½ pound smoked sturgeon, cut into 1-inch cubes
4 tablespoons butter
4 tablespoons flour
½ teaspoon celery seed
¼ teaspoon salt
2 cups milk
½ cup white Beaujolais (or other white wine)
2 hard-cooked eggs, chopped
½ cup bread crumbs
butter

Melt the butter in a small saucepan, gradually blend in the flour, celery seed, salt, and parsley. Stir until smooth and gradually stir in the milk. Cook, stirring until sauce thickens.

Preheat oven to 400 degrees.

Add the wine, eggs, and sturgeon to the sauce. Cook 5 minutes, then transfer to a shallow baking dish.

Sprinkle with bread crumbs, dot with butter, and bake 5 minutes, or until crumbs are brown.

4 SERVINGS

Vierend Eel

3 pounds eels, cleaned and cut into 4-inch pieces
juice of 1 lemon
3 tablespoons cognac
2 teaspoons salt
½ teaspoon pepper
1 egg, well beaten
½ cup milk
1 cup flour
fat for deep frying
chopped dill or parsley

Combine the lemon juice, cognac, 1 teaspoon salt, and ½ teaspoon pepper, and marinate the eels in this mixture for an hour or so, turning often.

Combine the egg and milk, sprinkle in the flour, add a teaspoon of salt, and mix into a smooth batter.

Dip the eel pieces into the batter and fry 2 or 3 at a time in deep fat until golden brown.

Serve garnished with chopped dill.

4 SERVINGS

Fish and Chips Harkness

4 fish fillets (sole, flounder, fluke, or any flat fish)
½ teaspoon salt
flour
2 eggs, lightly beaten
bread crumbs
cooking oil

Sprinkle the fillets with salt, roll first in flour then in egg, then in bread crumbs.

Place one at a time in a frying basket, and fry 3 to 5 minutes in 265-degree deep fat.

Serve with chips (French fried potatoes).

4 SERVINGS

Cupola Kippers

4 kippers, soaked overnight
2 eggs, well beaten
½ cup grated Cheddar cheese
½ cup butter
chopped parsley

Remove skin, heads, tails, and bones from the kippers (or use canned kippers) and dip them into the beaten eggs.

Sprinkle on both sides with grated cheese, then flour, and fry them 2 minutes on each side in butter over moderate heat (don't let the butter smoke).

Serve sprinkled with cheese and parsley.

4 SERVINGS

Sole Soleri

4 sole fillets (or other flatfish)
½ teaspoon salt
1 cup dry vermouth
¼ cup fish stock (or clam broth)
2 egg yolks
1 tablespoon heavy cream
pinch cayenne
1 cup butter, softened

Sprinkle the fillets with the salt, roll up, and fasten with toothpicks.

Poach gently in a mixture of the vermouth and stock for about 10 minutes or until fish flakes when fork-tested. Remove to an oven-proof serving dish and keep warm.

Boil down the cooking liquid to ¼ cup.

Place a bowl in a pan containing simmering water. Put in the remaining ingredients and the reduced liquid, and beat with a wire whisk until thickened and creamy.

Pour the sauce over the fillets and glaze under the broiler for a few minutes until sauce is golden.

4 SERVINGS

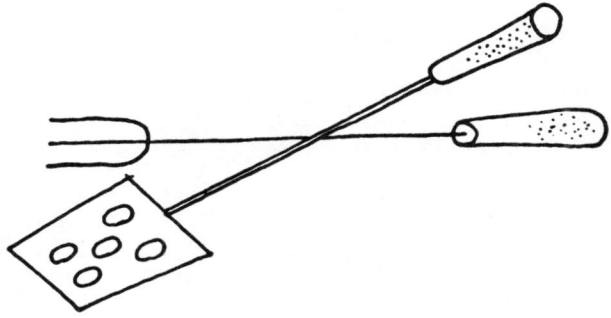

Blueprint Oysters Rockefeller Center

24 medium bluepoint oysters on the half shell
1 cup melted butter
¼ cup minced shallots (or scallions)
¼ cup minced celery
¼ cup minced parsley
1 cup minced watercress (or spinach)
1 clove garlic, minced
½ teaspoon dried chervil
½ teaspoon dried tarragon
¼ cup soft bread crumbs
few drops Worcestershire sauce
few drops Tabasco sauce
½ teaspoon salt

Preheat oven to 450 degrees.

Mix all the ingredients—except the oysters—together in a blender, or grind them in a mortar.

Make a bed of damp rock salt in a shallow baking dish, arrange the half-shell bluepoints on the salt, and place a spoonful of the sauce on each.

Bake until sauce bubbles (4 or 5 minutes). Serve at once.

4 SERVINGS AS A MAIN DISH, 8 AS AN APPETIZER

Crab Louis Sullivan

2 cups king crab (or other crab meat)
shredded lettuce
Louis Sullivan dressing
2 hard-cooked eggs, sliced
ripe olives
Louis Sullivan Dressing (see page 95)

Place the crab meat into a bed of lettuce in a chilled salad bowl, top with Louis Sullivan dressing, and garnish with sliced eggs and olives.

4 SERVINGS

Building Cod

4 codfish steaks (about 3 pounds)
1 tablespoon cooking oil
2 tablespoons lemon juice
4 tablespoons melted butter
½ cup dry white wine
4 scallions, finely chopped
½ teaspoon salt
½ teaspoon pepper (preferably white)
½ cup dry bread crumbs
½ cup grated cheese
1 teaspoon curry powder

Heat the oil in a heavy skillet, and sauté the steaks gently for 2 minutes on each side.

Combine the lemon juice, melted butter, wine, salt, and pepper, and add mixture to the skillet.

Cook the steaks 5 minutes longer, basting frequently with the sauce.

Combine the bread crumbs, cheese, and curry powder, and spread the mixture on the steaks.

Baste again, and place the skillet under the broiler for 2 to 4 minutes, or until top browns.

4 SERVINGS

Plat Nerwarren

1 dozen oysters, shucked
1 dozen sea scallops
1 dozen shrimp, shelled and deveined
1 egg, lightly beaten into 2 cups milk
bread crumbs mixed with flour
salt
pepper
fat for deep frying
lemon slices

Heat the fat to 365 degrees.

Dip the seafood into the milk-egg mixture, then into the crumbs-flour mixture.

Place in a wire basket a few at a time, and deep fry until golden. Serve with lemon slices and tartar sauce.
4 SERVINGS

Seafood Sea Ranch

2 cups cooked seafood (lobster meat, small shrimp, bay scallops, crabmeat, etc.)
¼ cup melted butter
1 tablespoon sherry
1 tablespoon brandy
1 cup cream
3 egg yolks, slightly beaten
salt
cayenne
nutmeg
4 slices toast

Cook the seafood in the butter for 3 minutes, then stir in the sherry and brandy.

Add the cream, egg yolks, and seasonings. Stir over low heat until thickened. Serve on toast.
4 SERVINGS

Vegetables and Side Dishes

Vegetables and Side Dishes

Candied Sweet's

4 medium-sized sweet potatoes
¼ cup butter
¼ cup brown sugar
¼ cup water

Boil the potatoes until tender but still firm. Peel and cut in half.

Heat the butter in a heavy skillet, stir in the sugar, and add the potatoes. Turn to cook on all sides, then add ¼ cup water. Cover the skillet, and cook over very low heat. Cook until tender and brown.

4 SERVINGS

Artichokes al Record

4 artichokes
creamed crab meat or chicken
bread crumbs
butter
grated American cheese

Wash the artichokes thoroughly, strip the stems close to the leaves, remove the tough outer leaves, and scissor off the prickly tops.

Place in a saucepan with 2 inches boiling water, and cook about half an hour, or until leaves pull off easily.

Preheat oven to 350 degrees.

Turn upside down, drain, and cut out the center choke; spread the leaves apart to make a cup.

Fill each artichoke with creamed crab or chicken; top with bread crumbs, a dab of butter, and cheese.

Place in a baking dish, cover, and cook half an hour. Uncover to brown tops.

4 SERVINGS

Sir Basil Spinach

2 cups chopped cooked spinach
4 tablespoons butter
1 tablespoon flour
salt and pepper
pinch basil
chopped almonds, sautéed in butter

Melt the butter, add the spinach, and cook 3 minutes, stirring.

Sprinkle with flour, season to taste with salt and pepper. Stir well, and serve sprinkled with almonds.

4 SERVINGS

Aaltomatoes

4 medium-sized tomatoes
1 cup bread crumbs
1 tablespoon chopped green pepper
1 tablespoon chopped onion
salt
pepper
4 teaspoons butter

Cut a slice from the stem-end of the tomatoes, remove the pulp and seeds. Invert and let stand half an hour or longer to drain.

Preheat oven to 400 degrees.

Mix together the bread crumbs, chopped vegetables, and seasonings. Stuff the tomatoes with this mixture, place a teaspoon of butter on each, and bake in a shallow buttered pan for 20 minutes.

4 SERVINGS

Corn-on-the-Corb

Remove tough outer husks from fresh ears of corn, pull back the inner husks and remove the silk. Replace inner husks.

Cook 5 minutes—no longer—in a boiling mixture of half milk and half water.

Serve with plenty of butter.

HUD Spuds

4 cooked potatoes, peeled and cut into 1-inch-thick slices
2 tablespoons melted butter
Mozzarella cheese

Preheat the broiler, brush the potatoes with butter, and place butter-side down on the grill. Broil until brown.

Turn, brush each slice again with butter, and cover with slices of cheese. Broil until cheese melts and bubbles.

Mobile Home Fried Potatoes

Wash and pare the potatoes; slice them thin, using a vegetable slicer for uniformity of thickness. Let stand half an hour in cold water, then drain and dry between towels.

Heat fat ½-inch deep in a heavy skillet and add a little minced onion (this is optional). Put in the potatoes, season with salt, and sauté over low heat about 15 minutes or until golden. Turn occasionally for uniformity of color.

Cover the skillet and cook 15 minutes longer until tender.

Vegetables and Side Dishes

Levittown Mushrooms

1 dozen large mushrooms, with stems removed
salt and pepper
butter
1 cup cream
4 slices toast

Preheat oven to 450 degrees.

Place the mushrooms smooth-side down in a buttered baking dish, sprinkle with salt and pepper, and dot with butter. Pour the cream around them, and bake uncovered 10 minutes.

Serve on toast with the juices over the mushrooms.

2 SERVINGS

Hominy Grids

1 cup hominy grits
4 cups water
1 teaspoon salt
2 tablespoons butter

Salt the water, and bring to a boil in a heavy saucepan. Add the grits slowly, stirring constantly.

Reduce the heat, cover the saucepan, and simmer slowly for half an hour, stirring from time to time. Stir in the butter, and serve.

4 SERVINGS

High Rice

2 tablespoons cooking oil
2 tablespoons butter
1 cup rice
2 cups hot consommé
1 teaspoon salt

Heat the oil and butter in a heavy skillet, and cook-stir the rice over low heat about 20 minutes, or until browned.

Stir in the consommé and salt, and bring to a quick boil. Reduce the heat, and simmer 20 minutes.

4 SERVINGS

I Beans

1 cup cooked pea beans
1 cup chicken broth
1 onion, finely chopped
6 pimentoes, finely chopped
¼ cup butter
1 teaspoon salt
1 teaspoon paprika

Preheat oven to 300 degrees.

Mix all the ingredients and put into a baking dish. Cover, and bake until broth is absorbed.

4 SERVINGS

Sauces and Dressings

"I'm going to ask the architect to reexamine our lines of flow. I'm tired of hearing her yell 'gangway' all the time."

Sauces and Dressings

Ebasco Sauce

½ cup meat skillet juices
½ cup dry white wine
1 teaspoon cornstarch
dash Tabasco

Add the wine to the skillet juices and bring to a boil. Stir in the cornstarch, Tabasco, and a little hot water. Stir until thickened.

1 CUP

Renaissauce

1 tablespoon butter
1 tablespoon flour
½ teaspoon salt
¼ teaspoon pepper
few grains cayenne
1 cup milk
3 tablespoons Dijon mustard
1 tablespoon fresh horseradish

In a small saucepan, melt the butter over low heat. Blend in the four and seasonings, stirring until mixture is smooth.

Remove from heat, stir in the milk, and boil 1 minute. Stir in the mustard and horseradish. Serve warm.

1 CUP

Louis Sullivan Dressing

½ cup olive or salad oil
10 stuffed olives, chopped
1 teaspoon minced onion
1 tablespoon minced parsley
¼ teaspoon dry mustard
½ teaspoon paprika
1 teaspoon salt
1 teaspoon Worcestershire sauce
juice of ½ lemon and ½ orange

Put all the ingredients into a jar, shake well and chill.

Quonset Hot Sauce

2 8-ounce cans tomato sauce
chopped jalapeños to taste
1 tablespoon oil
1 tablespoon vinegar
¼ teaspoon orégano
½ teaspoon salt

Mix all the ingredients together, and serve either hot or cold.

1 PINT

Sasaki, Dawson, De Mayonnaise

½ teaspoon dry mustard
½ teaspoon sugar
½ teaspoon salt
few grains cayenne
1 egg yolk (room temperature)
¾ cup salad oil (room temperature)
1 tablespoon vinegar
1 tablespoon lemon juice
8 sprigs watercress
8 leaves spinach
4 sprigs parsley

Sift together into a small deep bowl the mustard, sugar, salt, and cayenne. Mix in the egg yolk. Beat in the vinegar.

Using a rotary egg beater, blend in the oil a teaspoonful at a time until dressing is the consistency of whipped cream. Stir in 1 tablespoon lemon juice (more if mayonnaise is too thick). Set aside.

Cover the watercress, spinach, and parsley with boiling water, and let stand 10 minutes. Drain, and put into cold water. Drain again, and put through a fine sieve. Add greens to the mayonnaise and mix well.

ABOUT 1 CUP

Ralph Adams Cranberry Sauce

1 pound cranberries, washed
1½ pounds sugar
rind of 1 orange, chopped
2 cups boiling water

Mix all the ingredients together and simmer over low heat 15 minutes. Skim and cool.

6 SERVINGS

H. H. Rich Hard Sauce

½ cup butter
1 cup confectioners' sugar
2 teaspoons brandy
1 egg white, beaten until stiff

Blend the butter, sugar and brandy until smooth. Fold in the egg white. Chill for an hour before serving.

2 CUPS

Carl A. Morse Sauce

3 tablespoons pan drippings (with fat skimmed)
1 onion, chopped
1 green pepper, chopped
1 tomato, chopped
salt
pepper
1 teaspoon bread crumbs
1 cup water
4 tablespoons sour cream

Put the vegetables and seasonings in the drippings, and simmer 15 minutes.

Add the bread crumbs and water, simmer until smooth. Strain, stir in the sour cream, and serve in a gravy boat.

ABOUT 2 CUPS

McKim, Mead, and White Sauce

2 tablespoons butter
2 tablespoons flour
1 cup milk or half-and-half
salt and pepper

Melt the butter in a small saucepan over low heat. Stir in the flour and blend well with a wire whisk.

Add the milk and continue to blend until thickened and creamy. Cook 2 to 3 minutes and season to taste.

1 CUP

Bar-O-Que Sauce

1 teaspoon salt
1 teaspoon chili powder
1 teaspoon celery seed
¼ cup brown sugar
¼ cup vinegar
¼ cup Worcestershire
2 cups water
dash Tabasco

Mix all the ingredients together and simmer ½ hour.

3 CUPS

Desserts and Sweets

"Please! This is the work area, not the recreational area!"

Cottage Pudding

1½ cups all-purpose flour
1½ teaspoons baking powder
½ cup sugar
½ teaspoon salt
1 egg, beaten
½ cup milk
½ cup melted butter

Preheat oven to 400 degrees.

Sift all the dry ingredients together. Mix together the egg, milk, and butter.

Stir the milk mixture into the dry ingredients, and pour into a buttered cake pan.

Bake 20 minutes or until brown.

Serve topped with whipped cream, crushed fruit or your favorite sauce.

6 SERVINGS

UTAPioca Pudding

1 egg, lightly beaten
2 tablespoons tapioca
¼ cup brown sugar
¼ teaspoon salt
2 cups milk
¼ cup shredded coconut
½ teaspoon vanilla
whipped cream

Mix together all the ingredients.

Cook-stir over moderate heat until pudding boils, and tapioca is soft. Let stand 15 minutes.

Serve topped with a dab of whipped cream.

4 SERVINGS

Apple Pan Gaudi

3 cups tart apples, peeled and sliced
¾ cup brown sugar
¼ teaspoon nutmeg
¼ teaspoon cinnamon
¼ teaspoon salt
Cottage Pudding batter (see page 100)
whipped cream

Preheat oven to 350 degrees.

Put the apples into a buttered baking dish (1½ quart) and sprinkle with the seasonings.

Bake 15 minutes or until apples are soft.

Spread the batter on top and bake 20 minutes longer or until brown.

Cut into 6 squares and serve with crust on the bottom. Top with whipped cream.

6 SERVINGS

Eiffel Trifle

¼ cup cognac
¼ pound ladyfingers
½ cup Nesselrode sauce
whipped cream

Brush the ladyfingers with the cognac, and arrange in a serving bowl. Spread the Nesselrode sauce over the ladyfingers and garnish with whipped cream.

4 SERVINGS

Oeufs à la Netsch

2 egg whites
¼ teaspoon cream of tartar
½ cup sugar
2 cups milk
1 teaspoon vanilla
4 eggs, beaten
¼ cup sugar

Beat the egg whites and cream of tartar until foamy, then beat in the sugar a little at a time until stiff and glossy. Shape to resemble eggs.

In a saucepan, heat the milk to boiling, and add the vanilla. Drop in the meringue "eggs." Turn to poach evenly. Remove the "eggs" and drain on paper towel.

Strain the milk, add 4 eggs and ½ cup sugar. Cook and stir over low heat until thickened. Cool and spoon over the meringues.

6 SERVINGS

Morley Pears

2 large pears, peeled, split in half, and cored
4 scoops vanilla ice cream
1 cup raspberries (fresh, frozen, or canned), crushed
¼ cup sugar

Put a scoop of vanilla ice cream into each of 4 pear halves, and cover with sauce made by cooking a mixture of raspberries and sugar for 10 minutes.

4 SERVINGS

Plumb Pudding with H. H. Rich Hard Sauce

1 cup suet, finely chopped
2 cups dry bread crumbs
1 cup grated carrots
grated peel of 1 lemon
4 eggs yolks, well beaten
1½ cups brown sugar
2 tablespoons flour
1½ teaspoons salt
1 teaspoon cinnamon
½ teaspoon nutmeg
¼ teaspoon powdered clove
1 cup seedless raisins, chopped
¾ cup currants
4 egg whites, beaten until stiff
H. H. Rich Hard Sauce (see page 97)

Mix together the suet, bread crumbs, carrots, and lemon peel. Beat the sugar into the egg yolk, and add to the above mixture. Mix the flour, seasonings, raisins, and currants, and add to the above mixture.

Fold in the beaten egg whites and transfer to a buttered mold, filling no more than ⅔ full to allow for expansion. Cover tightly.

Place the mold on a rack in a deep kettle and add boiling water halfway up the mold. Cover tightly and steam 3½ hours.

Unmold and serve with H. H. Rich Hard Sauce.

8 SERVINGS

Peach Pie Portman

2 9-inch pie shells
2½ cups cooked dry peaches, chopped and sweetened
2 tablespoons flour
1 teaspoon cinnamon
½ cup brown sugar
pinch salt

Preheat oven to 450 degrees.

Line a 9-inch pie pan with a shell, and spoon in the peaches.

Sift together the flour, sugar, cinnamon, and salt, and sprinkle on top of the pie.

Put on the top crust, crimp the edges, and puncture with steam vents.

Bake about half an hour or until upper crust is golden.

José Luis DesSert

12 ounces semi-sweet chocolate
¾ cup light cream
3 tablespoons kirsch, Cointreau, or Triple Sec

In a heavy saucepan, melt the chocolate over low heat. Add the cream, and stir until smooth.

Remove from heat, stir in the liqueur, and pour into fondue pot or other heatable container. Keep warm, and use as a dip for marshmallows, lady fingers, strips of cake or fruit.

Desserts and Sweets

Yale A. & A. Flambé

2 cups canned black cherries, drained
1 tablespoon sugar
1 tablespoon cornstarch
1 cup cherry juice
½ cup brandy

Mix together in a chafing dish the sugar and cornstarch, and stir in the cherry juice a little at a time.

Cook-stir 3 minutes, then add the cherries. Warm the brandy, pour over the cherries, and ignite. Serve (over vanilla ice cream, if you wish) while flaming.

6 SERVINGS

Earl Flans Burgh

2 cups sugar
4 eggs
1 large can evaporated milk
1 teaspoon vanilla extract
3 tablespoons rum

Preheat oven to 350 degrees.

Put a cup of sugar into a small deep pan and heat, stirring, until sugar melts and turns golden. Tip the pan around until the sides are coated with the caramel. Cool.

Beat the eggs, add the milk, remaining sugar, and vanilla. Mix well, pour into the caramelized pan, and place in a larger pan containing hot water. Bake an hour or until a knife inserted in the center comes out clean.

Turn out onto a platter, pour on the warm brandy, ignite and serve while flaming.

4 SERVINGS

Cherry Turner Overs

2½ cups all-purpose flour
¼ teaspoon soda
½ teaspoon salt
½ cup butter
1 cup sugar
2 eggs
1 teaspoon vanilla
½ cup sugar
2 tablespoons cornstarch
2 tablespoons grated orange peel
1 cup maraschino cherries with syrup
1½ tablespoons butter

Mix together the dry ingredients.

Mix together the butter, sugar, eggs, and vanilla.

Blend the 2 mixtures, and chill ½ hour.

Meanwhile, mix together the sugar, cornstarch, orange peel, cherries, and butter. Cook-stir until mixture boils and thickens. Cool.

Preheat oven to 400 degrees.

Roll chilled dough on a floured board until 1/16-inch thick. Cut into 4-inch discs. Spoon cherry mixture onto half of each, fold dough over filling, and press edges together.

Place on a cookie sheet and bake 8 minutes or until lightly browned.

Fallingwater Melon

Cut a plug in a ripe watermelon and slowly pour in a pint of brandy, rum, or whisky. Turn the melon so that all parts might absorb the liquor.

Refrigerate for a few hours and serve sliced.

Paul Rhubarb Pie

1 cup sugar
2 tablespoons flour
1 egg, lightly beaten
3 cups chopped rhubarb
2 pie shells
½ cup raisins

Preheat oven to 450 degrees

Mix together the sugar and flour, stir in the egg, and then the rhubarb.

Line a 9-inch pie pan with one of the shells, spoon in the filling, and sprinkle the raisins on top.

Cover with the second shell, brush the edges of the first shell with water, and crimp the two edges together. Prick the top with a fork to allow steam to escape during the cooking.

Bake about 40 minutes, or until tender when fork-tested. If top crust browns too quickly, cover with brown paper.

Carnegie Melon

1 ripe cantaloupe
4 scoops ice cream
8 tablespoons crushed pineapple
4 ounces rum

Cut cantaloupe in half and remove seeds. Cut 2 1-inch-thick slices or rings from each half, and carefully cut off the rind.

Place a ring on each of 4 dessert plates and fill with ice cream. Top with crushed pineapple.

Warm the rum, ignite, and pour, flaming, over the melon.

William Morris Mallow Pudding

½ pound marshmallows
½ cup broken pecans or walnuts
¼ cup chopped maraschino cherries
1 tablespoon maraschino juice
½ pint whipping cream
2 tablespoons confectioners' sugar
1 teaspoon rum or sherry

Mix together the marshmallows, nuts, cherries, and juice.

Whip the cream, add the sugar and flavoring, and fold in the marshmallow mix.

Pour into a mold and refrigerate 2 or 3 hours until firm.

6 SERVINGS

Machu Peaches

6 peaches
chopped nuts
brown sugar
6 maraschino cherries
1 lemon
H. H. Rich Hard Sauce (see page 97)

Preheat oven to 350 degrees.

Dip peaches quickly in hot water and peel. Split in half and remove stones.

Place in a shallow baking dish cut-side up, and fill the cavities with chopped nuts and a little brown sugar.

Place a maraschino cherry on each, squeeze in a little lemon juice, and bake 20 minutes.

Serve with H. H. Rich Hard Sauce.

4 SERVINGS

Charles Rennie Mackintosh Apple Pie

2 uncooked pie crusts
6 to 8 mackintosh apples pared, cored, and sliced
½ cup brown sugar
¼ teaspoon salt
½ teaspoon cinnamon
¼ teaspoon ground nutmeg
1 tablespoon butter

Preheat oven to 450 degrees.

Line a 9-inch pie pan with one of the crusts and fill evenly with the apples, piling them higher in the center.

Mix together the sugar, salt, cinnamon, and nutmeg, and sprinkle evenly over the apples.

Dot with butter, brush the edges of the crust with water, and cover with second crust; crimp edges with the fingers and prick top with a fork to allow steam to escape.

Bake about 40 minutes or until apples are tender.

John Hancock Drops

1 can sweetened condensed milk
1 package dry white frosting mix
½ pound shredded coconut
½ cup chopped nutmeats

Preheat oven to 350 degrees.

Heat the milk in a saucepan over low heat, and stir in the remaining ingredients.

Drop the mixture by teaspoonfuls onto a greased baking sheet, and slide into the oven. Turn off the heat and leave the candy in the oven until it is well glazed.

Edward Larrabee Bon-Bons

2 cups sugar
1¼ cups water
⅛ teaspoon cream of tartar
2 tablespoons rum

Put the water and sugar in a saucepan and stir over low heat until sugar dissolves.

Add the cream of tartar and rum, cover, and boil 3 minutes. Do not stir. Insert a candy thermometer, and boil mixture until it reaches 238 degrees. Wipe away any crystals that may form on the sides of the pan.

Pour onto a sheet of wax paper and let stand until almost cool. Knead with the hands until smooth and creamy. Shape into balls. Cover with a damp cloth and let stand ½ hour or until firm.

1 POUND

Lally Pops

12 lollipop sticks
3 tablespoons butter
¾ cup corn syrup
½ cup sugar
few drops food coloring

Butter a cookie sheet and arrange the lollipop sticks on it.

In a heavy saucepan, mix together the butter, syrup, and sugar. Bring the mixture to a boil, reduce the heat, and simmer, stirring until a little syrup dropped into cold water separates into hard threads.

Remove from the heat, stir in the coloring, and drop by tablespoonfuls over the ends of the sticks.

Walnuts Wagner

¾ cup brown sugar
2 tablespoons rum
1 tablespoon maple syrup
1½ cups walnut meats
confectioners' sugar

Mix together the sugar, rum, and syrup, and add the walnut meats. Stir until well coated, roll in sugar, and put on wax paper to dry.

Hobart Bits

½ cup powdered skim milk
¼ cup chopped pecan meats
¼ cup maple syrup
sugar

In a mixing bowl, mix together the milk and nut meats. Add the syrup and stir until well blended.

Transfer to a sugared board and knead until creamy. Let stand until firm, then mold into bits and roll in sugar.

Maison Glacé Fillip

2 scoops vanilla ice cream
4 meringues
crushed pineaple
whipped cream
maraschino cherries

Press 2 meringues around each scoop of ice cream, and serve topped with crushed pineaple and whipped cream. Decorate with maraschino cherries.

Desserts and Sweets

Credit Crunch

½ pound blanched almonds, finely chopped
1 cup butter
1 cup sugar
8 ounces semi-sweet chocolate

Put the almonds in a pan and toast lightly.

Cook the butter and sugar over low heat until well blended. Add half the nuts, and cooked until candy thermometer reads 310 degrees.

Pour into a lightly buttered 8x8-inch pan and cool.

Melt the chocolate over low heat, stirring until smooth. Spread half the chocolate over the nut mixture, and sprinkle with half the remaining nuts. Cool.

Turn the candy pan upside down on wax paper, and spread candy with remaining chocolate and nuts.

Cool and break into crunchy bits.

Ghirardelli Squares

2 ounces unsweetened chocolate
3 tablespoons milk
3 tablespoons butter
½ cup chopped nutmeats

Melt the chocolate in the top of a double boiler. Stir in the milk, butter, and nuts. Heat, stirring, 10 minutes.

Spread evenly onto a buttered pan, cool until firm, and cut into 1-inch squares.

Breads, Cakes, and Cookies

"Well, shall we form a primary conversation group in the area for relaxation?"

Max Urbuns

1 package yeast dissolved in 1 cup warm milk
2 tablespoons softened butter
1 tablespoon sugar
1 teaspoon salt
2½ cups all-purpose flour

Preheat oven to 400 degrees.

Combine the yeast-milk mixture, butter, sugar, and salt. Gradually add the flour and beat well for 5 minutes. Add enough flour to make dough firm.

Knead and put into buttered muffin pans, filling each only ⅓ full. Let dough rise about an hour until it doubles in bulk, and bake 15 minutes or until browned.

ABOUT 20 BUNS

Blue Behrens Pancakes

1 cup milk
2 tablespoons melted butter
1 egg
1 cup all-purpose flour
1 teaspoon baking powder
½ teaspoon salt
½ cup blueberries

Mix together the milk, butter, and egg.

Sift the flour, baking powder, and salt.

Combine the two mixtures, add the blueberries, and beat lightly.

Cook on a greased griddle until golden on both sides.

6 TO 8 PANCAKES

Breads, Cakes and Cookies

Alfred De Vidonuts

2 cups flour
2 teaspoons baking powder
¼ teaspoon nutmeg
½ teaspoon cinnamon
½ teaspoon salt
½ cup milk
1 egg
½ cup sugar
2 tablespoons oil
fat or oil for deep frying

Sift together all the dry ingredients.

Mix together in a mixing bowl the milk, egg, sugar, and oil. Ldd the dry ingredients and additional flour, if needed, to make the dough soft but just firm enough to handle.

Put 4 inches of deep fat or oil into a deep-fat fryer and heat to 360 degrees.

Roll out the dough on a floured board to ½ inch in thickness, and cut with a floured doughnut cutter.

Slide the doughnuts down a spatula into the hot fat. Cook 3 or 4 at a time, turning to brown on both sides. Remove carefully with tongs, and drain on a paper towel.

20 DOUGHNUTS

Myron Gold Fingers

¾ cup softened butter
¾ cup confectioners' sugar
1½ cups all-purpose flour
2 eggs
1 cup brown sugar
2 tablespoons flour
½ teaspoon salt
½ teaspoon vanilla
3 tablespoons grated orange peel

Preheat oven to 350 degrees.

Cream the butter and confectioners' sugar, blend in the flour, and spread into a 9x13-inch baking pan. Bake 12 minutes.

Mix together remaining ingredients and spread over the cake layer. Bake 20 minutes longer, cool, and cut into 3x1-inch fingers.

30 FINGERS

Rococonut Cookies

3 ounces unsweetened chocolate
1 can sweetened condensed milk
2 cups shredded coconut
1 teaspoon vanilla

Preheat oven to 350 degrees.

In a heavy saucepan heat the chocolate and milk until chocolate melts. Do not boil.

Stir in the coconut and vanilla. Drop onto a buttered cookie sheet and bake about 8 minutes.

ABOUT 40 COOKIES

Ezra Stollen

1 package dry yeast dissolved in 1 cup warm water
½ cup sugar
1 teaspoon salt
2 eggs
½ cup butter, softened
2½ cups of all-purpose flour
½ cup slivered almonds
¼ cup chopped citron
¼ cup candied cherries
1 tablespoon grated lemon peel
melted butter
confectioners' sugar

Put the yeast, sugar, salt, eggs, and butter into a mixing bowl and beat well with an egg beater or electric mixer.

Beat in 1½ cups of the flour, and let the dough rise for about an hour.

Stir in the almonds, citron, cherries, and lemon peel, and enough additional flour to stiffen the dough until it becomes almost unmanageable.

Cover and refrigerate about an hour.

Place dough on a well-floured board, flatten and form into 2 ovals about 6 x 10 inches, flour well, and transfer to a greased baking sheet.

Brush each oval with melted butter, and fold each lengthwise in half and press folded edges together. Let rise again about an hour or until it doubles its size.

Preheat oven to 375 degrees.

Bake about half an hour or until golden brown. Brush with a frosting made by stirring confectioners' sugar into ¼ cup boiling water until thickened. Decorate with fruit and nuts.

2 STOLLEN

Denise Scott Brownies

2 ounces unsweetened chocolate
⅓ cup butter
1 cup sugar
2 eggs
1 teaspoon vanilla
½ cup all-purpose flour
½ teaspoon baking powder
½ teaspoon salt
½ cup chopped walnut meats

Preheat oven to 350 degrees.

Using a heavy saucepan, melt chocolate and butter over low heat. Remove from heat and stir in the sugar, eggs, and vanilla. Then stir in the remaining ingredients.

Spread on a cookie sheet and bake half an hour, or until dry on top and almost firm to the touch. Do not overbake.

Cool slightly and cut into 2-inch squares.

ABOUT 16 BROWNIES

Joseph Molitorte

4 egg whites
1 cup confectioners' sugar
4 egg yolks
½ cup chopped pecans
½ cup grated unsweetened chocolate
½ cup cracker crumbs
1 teaspoon baking powder
whipped cream

Preheat oven to 325 degrees.

Beat the egg whites until stiff, and beat in ¼ cup sugar.

Beat the egg yolks until thick, and beat in ¾ cup sugar.

Add the chocolate, cracker crumbs, and baking powder. Fold in the egg whites.

Spoon into a buttered pan, spread evenly, and bake 25 minutes. Cool, split into 2 layers, and put together with whipped cream between and on top.

6 SERVINGS

Bows Arts

2½ cups all-purpose flour
1 teaspoon baking powder
1 teaspoon salt
¾ cup butter, softened
1 cup sugar
2 eggs
1 teaspoon vanilla

Mix together the dry ingredients in a heavy saucepan.

Mix together the remaining ingredients.

Blend the two mixtures, cover with a cloth, and chill about an hour.

Preheat oven to 400 degrees.

Roll dough out on a floured board to about ½ inch thick and cut into ½-inch strips 14 inches long. "Tie" into bow ties. Form figure eights with a loop on the left, a loop on the right, an end on the left or the right. Press together in the middle. Place on a cookie sheet and bake 6 to 8 minutes.

ABOUT 30 BOWS

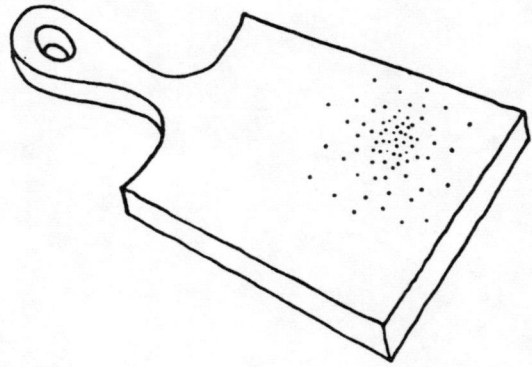

Tea Squares

1⅓ cups cake flour
2 teaspoons baking powder
¼ teaspoon salt
3 tablespoons softened butter
¾ cup sugar
½ teaspoon vanilla
1 egg, well beaten
½ cup milk
sugar

Preheat oven to 350 degrees.

Sift together the flour, baking powder, and salt.

Combine the butter, sugar, vanilla, and egg. Beat well, then gradually stir in the dry mixture.

Spoon into a buttered 8x8-inch pan. Sprinkle with sugar and bake. Cut into squares and serve warm.

Raisin Fees

1¼ cups flour
¼ teaspoon baking powder
¼ teaspoon salt
½ cup butter, softened
¾ cup sugar
1 egg
½ teaspoon vanilla
1 tablespoon cream
½ cup seedless raisins

Preheat oven to 375 degrees.

Sift together the flour, baking powder, and salt.

Mix together the butter, sugar, egg, vanilla, raisins, and cream.

Combine the two mixtures, drop teaspoonfuls onto a buttered cookie sheet, and bake about 8 minutes.

Inigo Scones

2 cups flour
2 teaspoons double-action baking powder
1½ tablespoons sugar
½ teaspoon salt
4 tablespoons softened butter
2 eggs, beaten
½ cup cream
sugar

Preheat oven to 450 degrees.

Sift into a mixing bowl the dry ingredients, and work in the butter.

Beat the egg and cream into the flour mixture. Add more flour if necessary. The dough should now be soft but firm enough to handle.

Turn out onto a floured board and knead. Roll into a flat rectangle ¾-inch thick, and cut into diamond-shaped scones. Brush with a little egg white diluted with water. Sprinkle with sugar and bake 15 minutes.

ABOUT 12 SCONES

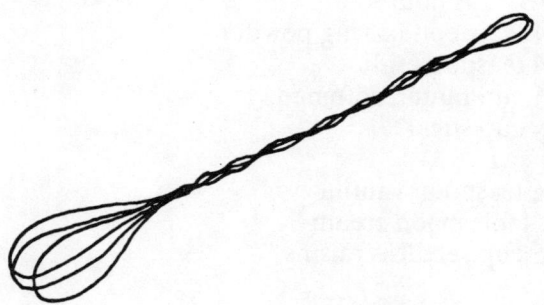

Beverages

"I think it's your new architect—they say he makes a thorough study of the owner's habits before designing a house—"

Bourbon Sprawl

1 lump sugar
2 dashes bitters
1 teaspoon water
1 ice cube
2 ounces bourbon whiskey
½ ounce anisette or Pernod
½ slice orange
twist of lemon peel
cherry

Put the sugar, bitters, and water into an old fashioned glass, and crush or stir. Add an ice cube, pour in the bourbon and anisette, decorate with orange, lemon, and cherry. Serve with a stirrer.

Canary Trace

1 ounce Galliano liqueur
6 ounces grapefruit juice
1 ounce vodka
4 ice cubes

Put all the ingredients into an old fashioned glass and stir.

Dome Perignon

1 ounce brandy
1 ounce Cointreau or Triple Sec
cracked ice
champagne
sprig of mint

Put the brandy and Cointreau into a 10-ounce highball glass half-filled with cracked ice, fill with champagne, and decorate with mint.

Mile-High Illinois

juice of ½ lemon
1 teaspoon sugar syrup
2 ounces gin
crushed ice
chilled champagne
slice of lemon
slice of orange
cherry

Put the lemon juice, syrup, and gin into a high 10-ounce glass. Stir, and fill with crushed ice.

Fill with champagne, decorate with lemon and orange slices and a cherry.

Brandy Alexandre Georges

1 ounce brandy
¾ ounce crème de caçao
¾ ounce sweet cream
cracked ice

Put all the ingredients into a cocktail shaker, and shake vigorously. Strain into a 4-ounce cocktail glass.

Rickey Franzen

½ lime
2 ounces gin
2 ice cubes
club soda, chilled

Squeeze the lime into an 8-ounce glass, and drop in the lime. Add 2 ice cubes and the gin. Stir, and fill with club soda. Stir again, but gently.

Indirect Lightning

3 ounces gin
dash French vermouth
twist of lemon
4 cubes of ice

Put all the ingredients into an old fashioned glass and stir vigorously until well chilled.

Building Types Toddy

1 egg yolk, beaten
1 ounce anisette
1 ounce curaçao
1 ounce brandy
hot water

Put the egg yolk, anisette, curaçao, and brandy into a tea cup, and fill with hot water. Stir.

Inflationary Squeeze

½ lime
2 ounces vodka
ginger beer
2 ice cubes

Squeeze the lime into a 10-ounce highball glass containing 2 ice cubes, and drop in the lime. Add the vodka, and fill with ginger beer. Stir gently.

Ionic Freeze

shaved ice
Metaxa
dash Pernod
Greek olive

Fill a 3-ounce cocktail glass with shaved ice, add a dash of Pernod, and fill with Metaxa. Stir until frosty, and decorate with a Greek olive.

A.W.N. Pugin Fizz

juice of ½ lemon
1 teaspoon sugar
1½ ounce gin
cracked ice
chilled club soda

Put the lemon juice, sugar, and gin into a cocktail shaker with cracked ice, and shake. Strain into an 8-ounce highball glass, and fill with chilled soda.

Café Perkins

1½ ounces whiskey
1 teaspoon sugar
strong, hot coffee
whipped cream

Put the whiskey, sugar, and coffee into a coffee cup, and stir until sugar is dissolved. Serve topped with whipped cream.

Meier's Rum Punch

2 ounces Myer's rum
juice of 1 lime
½ teaspoon curaçao
1 teaspoon sugar
cracked ice
shaved ice
slice of lime
stick of fresh pineapple

Put the rum, lime juice, curaçao, and sugar into a cocktail shaker with cracked ice and shake.

Strain into a 12-ounce glass filled with shaved ice, and decorate with lime and pineapple.

Colonnade

1 ounce brown crème de caçao
1 ounce green crème de menthe
1 ounce orange curaçao
1 ounce cherry liqueur
1 ounce brandy

Pour the ingredients, in the order given, into a sherry glass or straight-sided pony glass. Pour carefully off the back of a bar spoon so that each ingredient will form a well-defined layer.

Port Cochère

1½ ounces port wine
¾ ounces vodka
cracked ice
maraschino cherry

Stir the ingredients until well chilled and strain into a 3-ounce cocktail glass. Decorate with maraschino cherry.

Pile Driver

½ ounce white crème de menthe
1 ounce cognac
1 ounce cream
cracked ice

Put all the ingredients into a cocktail shaker, shake, and strain into a 3-ounce cocktail glass.

Spumante Bramante

1 lump sugar
2 dashes bitters
Asti Spumante "champagne," chilled
twist of lemon peel

Place the sugar in a 6-ounce champagne glass, dash in the bitters, and fill with Asti Spumante.

Rub the lemon twist around the edge of the glass, float it in the champagne, and serve.

Grand Coulee

2 tablespoons lemon juice
2 tablespoons sugar
crushed ice
maraschino cherry
sprig mint

Put the lemon juice, sugar, and water into a 10-ounce glass half-filled with crushed ice. Stir well to dissolve the sugar, fill with water, and decorate with a cherry and a sprig of mint.

Julep de Lesseps

about 12 sprigs mint
4 lumps sugar
shaved ice
8 ounces bourbon or rye whiskey

Put 4 tall glasses on a tray and set in the freezer until frosted.

Put a sprig of mint, a lump of sugar, and ½ ounce of whiskey in the bottom of each, and crush. Fill to the brim with ice and tamp down.

Add another ½ ounce of whiskey and stir with a long-handled spoon. Tamp down, and fill again with ice.

Pour in the remaining ounce of whiskey, tamp, and fill. Serve garnished with sprigs of mint.

4 DRINKS

Beverages

Bullfinch

1½ ounces vodka
½ ounce lemon juice
dash Worcestershire
dash Tabasco
pinch salt
dash pepper
cracked ice
beef broth

Put the vodka, lemon juice, and seasonings into a 10-ounce glass half-filled with cracked ice. Fill with beef broth and stir.

Greek Revival

juice of ½ lime
½ teaspoon sugar
2 dashes grenadine
1½ ounces Metaxa
cracked ice

Put everything into a cocktail shaker and shake well. Strain into a 3-ounce cocktail glass.

Herrera the Dog

Pour equal parts of chilled champagne and either stout or ale slowly and simultaneously into a tall glass.

Light My FAIA

4 teaspoons sugar
4 teaspoons water
finely crushed ice
4 jiggers heavy black rum
4 jiggers light rum
juice of 2 limes

Put a teaspoon of sugar and a teaspoon of water into each of 4 old fashioned glasses. Fill the glasses with ice, pour a jigger of black rum and a jigger of light rum into each, add lime juice, and stir.

4 DRINKS

OSHAke

2 ounces sake
dash Dubonnet
cracked ice

Stir the ingredients together until well chilled, and strain into a 3-ounce cocktail glass. Decorate with a twist of orange.

Menus

"Parker—what are all these lines of flow going to the bar?"

Menus

The recipes in *The Architectural Cookbook* can be combined into approximately 896,342 different menu combinations. In the interest of conservation, we are presenting eighteen suggested menus, which incidentally trace a professional career from B.Arch. to R.I.P. You will undoubtedly concoct favorite menus of your own, and in that endeavor we wish you a *Bon Appétit!*

Dinner to Honor a New Architectural Graduate

Meier's Rum Punch

Heroes Saarinen

Sole Soleri

Vol au Venturi

Yale A.&A. Flambé

Dinner to Celebrate Winning an Architectural Traveling Fellowship

Horta d'Oeuvres

Parthen on Toast

Flying Buttress of Pork with Spice/Thyme
Noodles Romanesque   Aaltomatoes

Apple Pan Gaudí

Menus

Dinner to Celebrate Getting Your First Job

Blueprint Oysters Rockefeller Center

Mullion Stew

Broiled Muntin Chops
Hominy Grids

Tea Squares

Canary Trace

Celebration Dinner for a Newly-Registered Architect

Light My FAIA

Chick Peas Marshall

Modulor Meatloaf with A1A Sauce
Candied Sweet's

Dome Perignon

Menus

Dinner to Celebrate Getting an Occupancy Permit for Your First House

Post and Lentil Soup

Lobster Thermi Door

Porter House Steak
Mobile Home Fried Potatoes   Levittown Mushrooms

Maison Glacé Fillip

Dinner to Celebrate First Publication of Your Work

Brandy Alexandre Georges

Baked Hughes with Herbs Smith   Artichokes al Record

Ezra Stollen   Joseph Molitorte

Morley Pears

Walnuts Wagner

Building Types Toddy

Menus

Dinner to Celebrate Winning the *Prix de Rome*

Pizza Piazza

Minestrone Michelangelo

Eternal Ziti   Linguine Bernini

St. Mark's Venison with Renaissauce

Spumante Bramante

Dinner on the Occasion of "Topping Out" a Major Building

Catenary Dip

Vierend Eel

Roast Beef au Joist
High Rice   I Beans

Lally Pops

Pile Driver

Menus

Luncheon Meeting With Financiers

No Risk Bisque

Capital Carp

Credit Crunch

Inflationary Squeeze

Luncheon Meeting with the Zoning Board

Suburban Spread   Cul-de-Snack

Chow Main Street

Building Cod

Cottage Pudding

Bourbon Sprawl

Menus

Dinner to Celebrate Winning a Lawsuit

Indirect Lightning

Eggs and Darts

Las Vegas Strip Steak		Nervi Noodles

Plumb Pudding with H.H. Rich Hard Sauce

John Hancock Drops

OSHAke

Dinner to Celebrate a Government Commission

Grand Coulee

Pot Luckman

Leg of Mitchell-Lama		HUD Spuds

Raisin Fees

Inflationary Squeeze

Menus

Dinner in Honor of a Chief Engineer

Julep deLesseps

F.W. Dodgepodge

Baltimore Trussed Chicken

Lamb LeMessurier with Ebasco Sauce

Eiffel Trifle

Mile-High Illinois

Dinner in Honor of Visiting Members of R.I.B.A.

Rabbit Adam

Sturgeon Soane

John Nash Hash   Sir Basil Spinach

William Morris Mallow Pudding

Inigo Scones   Charles Rennie Mackintosh Apple Pie

A.W.N. Pugin Fizz

Menus

An Architectural School's 25th Reunion Dinner

Carnegie Melon

Bauhaus Chowder

Moore Pork Sausages with Potatoes

Yale A.&A. Flambé

Canary Trace

Luncheon to Celebrate Your Firm's 10,000th Commission

Park Avenue Canopies

Emery Broth

SOMelette Parmentier

Fish Tishman

Café Perkins

Menus

Dinner to Celebrate One of Your Buildings Being Named a Landmark

Dome Perignon

Eclectic Stew

Bass Gilbert with McKim, Mead, and White Sauce

Carrère Roast Beef with Hastings Pudding

Port Cochère

Architect's Retirement Dinner

Ionic Freeze

Eternal Ziti

Cloister Stew

Lamb Cheops with Pediment Jelly

Bows Arts

Colonnade

Our thanks for recipe names and other suggestions
for *The Architectural Cookbook* to
Gerald Allen, Grace M. Anderson, Denise Scott Brown
(Venturi and Rauch), Kenneth DeMay (Sasaki, Dawson,
DeMay Assocs., Inc.), Hugh S. Donlan, Martin Filler,
William B. Foxhall, Barclay F. Gordon,
Joseph D. Holbrook, Jack R. Horstmeyer,
Blake Hughes, William Marlin, Philip J. Meathe
(Smith, Hinchman & Grylls Assocs., Inc.),
Richard Meier and Associates, Frowis E. Roewer
(Huygens and Tappé Inc.), Herbert L. Smith, Jr.,
Sir Basil Spence, O.M., Robert Venturi
(Venturi and Rauch), Jonathan Wagner,
Walter F. Wagner, Jr., and to Nancy Hawkins
for testing recipes.